Mediaeval
Feudalism

By CARL STEPHENSON

Cornell Paperbacks

Cornell University Press

ITHACA AND LONDON

SINCE its first printing in 1942 the late Carl Stephenson's *Mediaeval Feudalism* has enjoyed a distinguished career. Eminent historians of America and Europe have reviewed it with high praise in the most respected historical journals. To the college freshman it has been *a vade mecum* in the awesome task of mastering such complicated feudal principles as subinfeudation and liege homage. The omniscient graduate student has at first reading whisked through it with disdain, casting it aside for the imaginative hypotheses of a Marc Bloch or for the impressive tomes of German historians, only to come meekly back to it to obtain his bearings and a sense of proportion. Seasoned scholars and teachers have read the book with discrimination, realizing that behind each page stood years of research and thought devoted to the study of feudalism in mediaeval Europe; they in turn have recommended it to their students.

In this book, deceptively simple in its ease of explication, Professor Stephenson has digested the vast body of writings on feudalism, supplemented it with his own research, and then presented the subject with conclusions, observations, and suggestions that must be read through by anyone who hopes to understand mediaeval feudalism. Upon reading the book Carl Becker penned a note to his good friend Carl Stephenson which the latter proudly acknowledged as the highest compliment to his scholarship. After praising the style, Becker, himself an unsurpassed stylist, wrote that such a simple and straightforward book could be written only after its subject had been completely mastered. By reprinting *Mediaeval Feudalism* Cornell University Press has made a small classic readily available to a large body of nonacademic readers within whose comprehension it lies.

Regarded as one of America's foremost mediaevalists at the time of his death in 1954, Carl Stephenson had a long and significant scholarly career. A student of Charles Gross and Charles Homer Haskins at Harvard, he later studied with the renowned Henri Pirenne of Belgium and established close scholarly ties with such eminent mediaevalists as Professors Ganshof, Galbraith, Halphen, Prou, and Frölich. Most of his teaching was done at the University of Wisconsin and at Cornell, where he wrote his well-known books and articles.

Interested only in what the document said and bitterly opposed to easy theorizing and glib generalization, Carl Stephenson did his best work on those institutions found in mediaeval Europe between the Loire and the Rhine; this area where influences spilled back and forth over feudal boundaries lent itself to the comparative method wherein lay his strength and contribution to mediaeval scholarship. Writing far removed from western Europe and its acrimonious academic feuding, he dispassionately demolished much of the prejudiced nationalistic writing devoted to praising or damning Germanic or Latin institutions. His greatest joy came from demonstrating that a tax, a commune, or seignorialism and feudalism were not peculiar to one area but were common to all western Europe; they developed not as products of racial genius but in response to basic social, economic, and political requirements of the Middle Ages.

For fifteen years Carl Stephenson regularly published articles in the leading historical journals of America, England, Belgium, and France and established himself as an authority on taxation, representative assemblies, and the origin of urban institutions. His most mature work, *Borough and Town*, appeared in 1933; here he combined his research with scholarly methods developed on the Continent to show that the English borough was not an insular peculiarity but that it was like its continental counterpart in origin and constitution. He then turned his attention to seignorial and feudal institutions, work resulting in further articles and this book.[1] Along with these scholarly achievements Carl Stephenson found time to write a mediaeval history that yet remains the foremost college text and to collaborate on a book containing translations of English constitutional documents.

Those who but casually knew Carl Stephenson could never understand how such a skeptical and aloof man could write so vividly and sympathetically on historical subjects. This seemingly improbable accomplishment appeared even more paradoxical when attained by one riveted to hard and demonstrable evidence, writing about a historical age that has been more romanticized than

---

[1] For a fuller appreciation of Carl Stephenson's scholarly career and for reprints of his most significant articles, see *Mediaeval Institutions: Selected Essays,* ed. Bryce D. Lyon (Ithaca, N.Y.: Cornell University Press, 1954).

any other period. But to those privileged few who were permitted to know the real man and to learn how he functioned, these contradictions transformed themselves into supporting buttresses. A belligerent opponent of romantic history and fine theories resting upon insufficient evidence, the practical skeptic zestfully toppled such writing and pored over the available records to determine exactly what could be concluded about a historical institution or problem. When satisfied that he was working upon sound evidence and that all the facts had been assembled, he turned to the task of reconstruction. At this moment occurred the metamorphosis. With the enthusiasm and feeling of the artist and, yes, with the buoyancy of the boy with his kite on a fresh and early April morning, he built his facts into the articles and books that have stimulated the admiration and envy of all who can appreciate first-class historical thinking presented in a style that meets its high demands.

Perhaps Carl Stephenson had too little patience with those who differed with him, and perhaps there were not enough historical "grays" in his conclusions, but his predominant "blacks" and "whites" were honestly supported by the facts that he wove into a far more lively and realistic history than many of his protagonists—the Victorian romantics and the scientific fence-sitters—could produce.

To paraphrase the pages that follow would be an injustice to all who have not read this book and who are entitled to have the basic ingredients of mediaeval feudalism explained to them by a master. With the wider distribution that the new format will give, many new readers will be lured into the Middle Ages and, like the English historian Maitland with respect to Stubbs's *Constitutional History of England*, will be ready victims of a book not because they were "set to read it" but because they found it on a shelf and "read it because it was interesting."

University of Illinois
July 1956

BRYCE D. LYON

Preface

IN THE FOLLOWING *pages I have tried to explain,
as simply and concisely as possible, the historical
significance of the feudal system. Despite the
obvious importance of the subject, there has been
almost no general treatment of it in English to
supplement the brief statements of the ordinary
textbook. This small volume is intended to provide such a treatment—one which, it is hoped,
will prove useful to many college teachers.*

*My purpose has not been to give a comprehen-
sive description of Europe in the feudal age, or
even of feudal society. I have taken for granted
that the reader will be familiar with the main
political events of the Middle Ages: the barbarian
invasions, the formation of the Carolingian Empire, the establishment of the later monarchies,
the crusades, and the like. I have omitted all but
cursory mention of the manorial system and
the revival of commerce, admirable sketches of
which have already been published. I have, in
other words, restricted the discussion to the few
institutions that may be said to have constituted*

*feudalism proper or to have been peculiarly asso-
ciated with it. Four of the six chapters, dealing
with feudal custom when it enjoyed its greatest
vigor, are designed to introduce not only the
fundamental principles but also, by citing specific
cases, the actual working of the system. A wide
variety of other examples can, of course, be
readily found. More advanced students may perhaps be inspired to look for some of them, or will
accept the hints in the last chapter as a challenge
to further study of feudal decadence.*

*For many of the ideas set forth below I, like
every worker in the field, am largely indebted to
the scholarship of other historians, both living
and dead. Any one interested in an appreciation
of their writings is referred to my article, "The
Origin and Significance of Feudalism,"* Amer-
can Historical Review, *XLVI, 788–812. More
particularly, however, I wish to express my
thanks to Professor Sidney Painter of Johns
Hopkins University for the useful suggestions
made after his reading of my manuscript and
to Miss Julia E. Edmonson for her clever and
sympathetic drawing of figures in the Bayeux
Tapestry.*

Cornell University   CARL STEPHENSON
January, 1942

Contents

xi

Chapter One

THE ORIGINAL FEUDALISM

❧

NEITHER the English word "feudalism" nor its equivalent in French seems to have come into use until the later eighteenth century—after the Revolution of 1789 had turned scholarly attention to certain prominent features of the Old Régime. Since then "feudalism," "feudal system," and the like have become part of the historian's ordinary vocabulary; for such expressions are very convenient when we refer to the complicated relationships of past ages. But, unhappily for a student who first approaches the subject, modern writers have by no means adopted a consistent usage. Some call one group of institutions essentially feudal, some another. For many writers the adjective remains exceedingly vague—so vague that they have been led to discover feudal stages in the history of various peoples, beginning with the ancient Egyptians

The term "feudalism"

1

and coming down to the Japanese of a century ago.

Sociological comparison of this sort, however valuable it may be, has no place in the following sketch. The present object is to explain, as precisely as the sources permit, the institutions for which men of the Middle Ages coined the term "feudal." And although we shall eventually arrive at certain conclusions with regard to feudalism and its historical significance, we may profitably avoid all preliminary generalization. Even the matter of terminology may be left for discussion at the appropriate time. Without trying to decide in advance what was and what was not feudal, we can forthwith begin our survey of actual customs in the early mediaeval period.

The
comitatus

In the second century after Christ the Roman historian Tacitus wrote an essay which he called *Germania*, and which has remained justly famous. He declares that the Germans, though divided into numerous tribes, constitute a single people characterized by common traits and a common mode of life. The typical German is a warrior. Leaving the management of his home and the tillage of his fields to slaves and womenfolk, he devotes himself to war or, in default of such excitement, to loafing, drinking, and gambling. The rulers of the Germans are military leaders. Their assemblies are military gatherings. Except when armed, they perform no business, either private or public. But it is not their custom that any one should assume arms without the formal approval of the tribe. Before the assembly the youth receives a shield and a spear from his father, some other relative, or one of the chief men, and this gift corresponds to the *toga virilis* among the Romans—making him a citizen rather than a member of a household. Such recognition may come to the youth on account of his noble birth or the renown of his ancestors. Even so, he is likely to get his training in arms among the companions (*comites*) of a distinguished chieftain (*princeps*). Here birth counts for less than warlike prowess; for each companion emulates the other members of the band, and each chieftain strives to excel his rivals through the loyalty of his followers. On the battlefield it is shameful for the chieftain to be surpassed in bravery, or for the companions to be less brave than he. One who survives the leader in battle is doomed to lifelong disgrace; to defend and support him, glorifying him by valorous deeds, is the sacred obligation of all his companions. In return they expect military equipment, food, and a share of whatever booty may be won.

The importance of this vivid account by Tacitus lies in the fact that within the next five hundred years Germanic peoples had overrun the western provinces of the Roman Empire and there established a series of kingdoms that were long to dominate the European scene. Most of these peoples, for all their intermixture with the native population and their borrowing of Roman institutions, remained fundamentally barbarian. Much of their traditional custom, especially that which dictated the life of the warrior class, retained its ancient vigor. In that respect the testimony of the *Germania* is confirmed and amplified by countless writings of the early Middle Ages. For example, the warlike organization that Tacitus called the *comitatus* is heard of again and again in the later centuries—among the Goths, the Franks, the Lombards, the Anglo-Saxons, and even the Vikings of Scandinavia. The brave *comes* who fights and dies beside his *princeps* unquestionably reappears in the heroic *gesith* or *thegn* of the Anglo-Saxon epics.[1] It has, indeed, been conjectured that the actual German word translated by Tacitus as *comes* was an older form

---

[1] See especially *Beowulf* and the *Song of Maldon*.

of *gesith*, which literally means a companion on a journey. However that may be, the personal relationship thus found to have persisted among the Germanic conquerors of the Roman provinces was highly honorable to both parties. When the free warrior, to whom the bearing of arms was itself a mark of distinction, became the follower of a chieftain, he did so voluntarily and with the expectation of maintenance befitting his rank. He suffered no degradation. Nor did he of necessity bind himself for life. The tie could be readily broken by mutual consent. The youth who joined a band for the sake of adventure and experience might well hope on some future day to have a following of his own; for any man of adequate wealth and fame would naturally attract companions.

No relationship of this sort can be found among the Romans of the later empire. In their *Commendation* eyes the profession of arms, far from being the equivalent of gentility, was hardly respectable. Because most citizens had long avoided military service, the legions were recruited from among the residents of frontier territories, chiefly men of barbarian descent. The household troops with whom all great persons came to surround themselves were mercenaries of ignoble origin, if not actually servile. According to long-established custom, a lesser freeman could become the client of any wealthy Roman who agreed to be his patron. The client, however, was essentially an economic dependant; in return for gifts of money, food, and clothing, he helped to swell his patron's retinue on public occasions. Clientage, involving no military service and implying anything but social equality, was utterly unlike the Germanic *comitatus*. And the dissimilarity remained even after the Roman institution had spread among the Frankish conquerors of Gaul. There, under the Merovingian kings, we often hear of poor men who, in order to obtain the means of livelihood, commended themselves for life to some powerful person. The one who commended himself thus became the man (Latin *homo*, French *homme*) of a lord [2] (Latin *dominus* or *senior*, French *seigneur*). But none of these terms necessarily denoted a military relationship. Throughout the Middle Ages a lord's men included his serfs and peasants of all grades, as well as his armed retainers.

Meanwhile another institution of the later em-

---

[2] Derived from the Anglo-Saxon *hlaford*, or "loaf-keeper"; i. e., the head of a household or other person in authority.

pire had come to be widely extended by the barbarian rulers of the western provinces. This was the *precarium* or *precaria*, a grant of land to be held by some one during the pleasure of the donor. Under Roman law such a "precarious" tenure could be terminated at any time. Later, especially in the Frankish kingdom, it became a legal right of occupation for a period of years or for life, in return for the payment of rent or the performance of a stipulated service. The term *precaria* implied that the land had been obtained through the prayer (*preces*) of the recipient; but the grant might also be styled a benefice, because it was a boon (*beneficium*) on the part of the grantor. The words, again, are of minor significance. The important fact is that the typical benefice was an agrarian estate—a group of lands organized for production, with the appurtenant buildings, tools, domestic animals, and cultivators of the soil, both free and servile. As the result of an economic decline that had been under way for at least five hundred years, commerce had ceased to be an important source of wealth throughout most of the west. State and society were dominated by agriculture. The population tended to be sharply divided into two

The precaria and the benefice

classes: an aristocracy of landlords and an economically dependent peasantry. The holder of a benefice belonged to the former.

Carolingian vassalage

When, in the eighth century, the Austrasian mayors of the palace acquired first the control and then the sovereignty of the Frankish kingdom, these various customs, Roman or Germanic, had long been recognized as established law. Charles Martel, Pepin, and Charlemagne, faced with the need of defending and administering an enlarged kingdom, developed whatever usages they found advantageous. And it is in their official enactments that vassalage first appears as a prominent institution. Since the name and all that it denoted remain matters of controversy, one should not be too dogmatic on the subject. The following explanation is merely what, to the author at least, seems best to agree with the sources.

In the earlier Middle Ages we find numerous words for "boy" that might be used to designate either a slave, a free servant, or a military retainer: the Latin *puer;* the Germanic *degan* (Anglo-Saxon *thegn*); the Germanic *knecht* (Anglo-Saxon *cniht*, later *knight*); and the Celtic *gwas* (French *vassal*, Latinized as *vassus* or *vassalus*). And it is a remarkable fact that in three cases—*thegn, knight,* and *vassal*—the honorable implication became exclusive. Among the Anglo-Saxons *thegn* entirely superseded *gesith;* among the Franks *vassal* entirely superseded the old German expressions, one of which seems to have been *gasind.* Whatever the reason for the change in terminology—and complete lack of evidence makes it idle to indulge in speculation—the Frankish sources of the eighth and ninth centuries are filled with references to vassals. Those of the king enjoyed special honor throughout the Carolingian Empire. They were frequently employed on governmental missions. Most important, they constituted the élite of the army, serving as heavy-armed cavalry and often leading contingents of their own vassals into battle. To enable them to bear the expense of such obligations, they were usually endowed with benefices—estates which were carved out of the royal domain, or out of confiscated property of the church, and which were held on condition of providing the desired service. Vassals of persons other than the king, though often poor and less highly privileged, seem always to have been fighting-men *par excellence* and, as such, to have ranked far above ordinary peasants.

By examining various customs of the Carolingian period we have necessarily concerned our-
selves with the development of the institutions
called feudal. Before we proceed further, it might
be well to summarize the problem of that development through a series of questions and suggested answers.

(1) *What was the origin of vassalage?* Since
under the Carolingians, as in the later period,
vassalage was an honorable relationship between
members of the warrior class, to derive it from
the Romans seems quite impossible. In spite of
all the Latin words that came to be adopted by
the Franks in Gaul, mediaeval vassalage remained
essentially a barbarian custom, strikingly akin to
that described by Tacitus as the *comitatus*.[3] Originally this custom was shared by various Germanic peoples, notably the Anglo-Saxons. The
peculiarity of Frankish vassalage resulted, in the
main, from the governmental policy of the Carolingian kings.

(2) *What was the Carolingian policy with
regard to vassalage?* The Merovingian kingdom
had been at most a pseudo-Roman sham. By the
end of the seventh century it had utterly disin-
tegrated. The Carolingian kingdom was a new

---

[3] See below, pp. 21–22, 51.

unit created by the military genius of Charles Martel, Pepin, and Charlemagne. To preserve and strengthen their authority, these rulers depended less on their theoretical sovereignty than on the fidelity of their personal retainers, now styled vassals. So the key positions in the army, as well as the more important offices in church and state, came to be held by royal vassals. Eventually the rule was adopted that every great official, if not already a royal vassal, had to become one. The Carolingian policy, as will be seen in the following pages, utterly failed; yet it established legal precedents that were observed for many centuries.

(3) *What was the origin of the fief?* In Frankish times, as later, *beneficium* remained a vague *The fief* term. Various kinds of persons were said to hold benefices, and in return for various kinds of service or rent. Since the benefice of a vassal was held on condition of military service, we may call it a military benefice. At first there was no technical Latin word for such a benefice, though in the Romance vernacular it became known as a *feos* or *fief*.[4] This name, Latinized as *feodum*

---

[4] Derived from a Germanic word meaning cattle or property. Cf. the English "fee," which may denote any payment for service or, more technically, a fief (as in the expression "knight's fee").

or *feudum*, ultimately came into official use and so provided the root for our adjective "feudal" (French *féodal*). Whether or not the military benefice existed before the eighth century is still disputed. In any case, it was the Carolingians who made that form of tenure into a common Frankish institution, and the best explanation of their policy is the one presented by Heinrich Brunner. According to his famous thesis, the old Frankish army had been largely made up of infantry—of ordinary freemen who provided their own weapons and served without pay. In the eighth century, as the experience of warfare proved the insufficiency of the traditional system, the Carolingians anxiously sought to enlarge their force of expert cavalry. And to do so they developed what we know as feudal tenure by associating vassalage with benefice-holding.

(4) *What was the nature of the fief?* In its essence, we may say, a military benefice or fief was the special remuneration paid to a vassal for the rendering of special service. If the rulers had been able to hire mounted troops for cash, recourse to feudal tenure would have been unnecessary; for the Carolingian fief was primarily a unit of agrarian income. To call a fief a piece of land is inaccurate. What value would bare

acres have for a professional warrior who considered the work of agriculture degrading? Being the possession of a gentleman, the fief included organized manors, worked by the native peasantry according to a customary routine of labor.[5] Nor was this all. To hold a fief was also to enjoy the important privilege that the Carolingians knew as immunity. Within his own territory the royal vassal, like the clerical immunists of an earlier time, administered justice, collected fines and local taxes, raised military forces, and exacted services for the upkeep of roads, bridges, and fortifications. To some extent, therefore, he was a public official, a member of the hierarchy whose upper ranks included dukes, marquises, counts, and the greater ecclesiastics. As all these magnates came to be royal vassals, their offices, together with the attached estates, naturally appeared to be their fiefs. And as royal vassals passed on bits of their own privilege to subvassals, feudal tenure became inseparable from the exercise of political authority.

(5) *What, then, was the original feudalism?* In this connection we can do no better than quote

---

[5] See Miss Neilson's admirable sketch, *Medieval Agrarian Economy*, in the *Berkshire Studies in European History* (New York, 1936).

a shrewd observation by Ferdinand Lot: "It has become accepted usage to speak of 'feudalism,' rather than of 'vassalage,' from that point in history when, with rare exceptions, there were actually no vassals without fiefs." [6] By "feudalism," in other words, we properly refer to the peculiar association of vassalage with fief-holding that was developed in the Carolingian Empire and thence spread to other parts of Europe. Insofar as this association was effected for governmental purposes, feudalism was essentially political. It should not be thought of as a necessary, or even usual, stage in economic history. Although feudal institutions presupposed certain agrarian arrangements, the latter were not themselves feudal. The manorial system could prevail for centuries in a particular country, as it did in Britain, without leading to the feudalization of any local state. Nor should feudalism be described as a sort of anarchical force because its growth coincided with the disintegration of the Carolingian Empire. For reasons now to be considered, the more accurate statement is that feudalism became the basis of a new political organization—one that naturally emerged as an older system fell in ruins.

---

[6] In the series edited by G. Glotz, *Histoire générale: Histoire du Moyen Age*, I (Paris, 1928–34), 676, n. 188.

Chapter Two

PRINCIPLES OF FEUDAL TENURE

FROM the troubled history of the ninth and tenth centuries one truth clearly emerges: that the economic conditions which had come to prevail throughout western Europe made it impossible for any but a small state to survive. The Carolingian Empire proved too big to be effectively administered, especially when assailed on all sides by Vikings, Saracens, and Hungarians. The partition of 843 failed to bring a permanent improvement. Lothair's central kingdom was first broken into three parts and then, despite the persistence of several royal titles, into many more. To the east the kingdom of Louis the German was resolved into a group of autonomous duchies, which continued to defy the ambitions of the Saxon and Franconian emperors. To the west the kingdom of Charles the Bald became a mere tradition as all real authority passed to the local

Political developments in the ninth and tenth centuries

15

princes, lay and ecclesiastical. The Capetian accession made no essential change in the political structure of the country. Hugh Capet and his immediate successors attempted to govern only their hereditary principality—the march of Neustria, now virtually reduced to the Île de France. The rest of their theoretical kingdom was divided into a large number of similar units, among which the more important were Toulouse, Gascony, Aquitaine, Brittany, Anjou, Blois, Champagne, Burgundy, Flanders, and Normandy. Some of these principalities were of Carolingian, some of more recent, creation. Whatever their legal origin, force had played a large part in their development; and force continued to govern their destinies. The most successful were those whose rulers maintained the best armies and the strongest administrations.

In such an environment feudal institutions continued to thrive because they provided a very simple and practical means of government. For the same reason they eventually spread across the continent of Europe, from the British Isles to Syria. It is therefore a matter of great historical interest to discover how feudal institutions actually worked in the various regions where they were adopted, and how they were transformed by political developments in the subsequent age. Before we examine particular states, however, we must have a clear understanding of feudal custom in general. This understanding, in spite of all local variation, is not hard to obtain. By disregarding the legal compromises and distinctions of later centuries, we may readily perceive a substratum of common usage—a set of principles that, being traceable to Carolingian times, we recognize as fundamental.

The original feudalism, as we have already seen, arose from the association of fief-holding with vassalage. Of these two the latter was the basic element. The Carolingian capitularies frequently refer to unbeneficed vassals who lived in their lords' households; and although such vassals became exceptional in the following period, it was always possible for a man to become a vassal without receiving a fief. On the other hand, a fief could legally exist only when held by a vassal. This fact, too often overlooked, demands a few words of explanation. Not every benefice, it should be remembered, was a fief; nor was every free tenant a vassal. Land held at rent, like the old *precaria*, the French called a *censive*, and to it the law of feudal tenure did not apply. A man who performed agricultural

The personal character of vassalage

service, whatever his ancestry, was doomed to be a peasant rather than a vassal because he was not of the military class. Besides, as will be more clearly shown below, the fief of a deceased vassal did not come into the lawful possession of his heir until the latter had himself acquired the status of vassal. Although fiefs might be declared hereditary, vassalage, remaining a wholly personal relationship, could never be inherited.

Homage and fealty

To become a vassal, a man (B) had to appear before his future lord (A) and render to him the service technically called homage (Latin *homagium*, from *homo*) and fealty (Latin *fidelitas*). B knelt, placed his hands between those of A, and acknowledged himself A's man, pledging entire faith as a vassal to his lord against all men who might live or die.[1] In equally formal words A accepted B's homage, raised him to his feet, and, as a rule, kissed him. Finally, on the Gospels or on sacred relics, B took a solemn oath to confirm his earlier promise. There was never, of course, an absolute uniformity of usage, and with the elaboration of feudal tenure numerous differences were introduced in the spoken formulas.

---

[1] See the examples published by E. P. Cheyney in *Translations and Reprints from the Original Sources of European History* (Dept. of History, U. of Pennsylvania, 1898), IV, no. 3, pp. 18–21.

But the act of homage remained essentially the same, and it was always followed, never preceded, by the oath of fealty.

Here, it should be remarked, we are dealing with two phases of a single ceremony rather than with two ceremonies. At most the oath of fealty gave Christian sanction to an obligation implicit in homage; for nobody could become a vassal without promising to be faithful to his lord. We have positive evidence that, as early as the eighth century, homage was a well-known Frankish custom. Presumably it was much older. The kernel of the ceremony, we may suspect, was barbarian and heathen, originally a form of admission into the chieftain's band of companions; ecclesiastical influence must have added the oath of fealty. The latter, in any case, could not of itself create the bond of vassalage. During the Carolingian age, as at a later time, the free subjects of a ruler could be required to swear fealty to him without the slightest thought of their becoming his vassals. Our conclusion must therefore be that fealty did not imply homage, but that homage did imply fealty. We may, indeed, follow the example set by numerous official documents and, speaking of homage alone, take its regular sequel for granted.

The preceding argument is supported by the fact that, although the lord took no oath of fealty, he pledged himself to a great deal by accepting a man's homage. The Frankish capitularies, which refer only indirectly to the vassal's obligation of keeping faith, carefully specify the ways in which he may be wronged by his lord. According to an edict of Charlemagne,[2] a vassal is justified in deserting his lord for any one of the following reasons: if the lord seeks to reduce him to servitude, if the lord plots against his life, if the lord commits adultery with his wife, if the lord attacks him with drawn sword, or if the lord fails to protect him when able to do so. Two centuries later Fulbert, bishop of Chartres, stated the same principle in a famous letter to the duke of Aquitaine.[3] Fulbert declares that one who swears fealty to his lord should, in order to deserve his benefice, faithfully give aid and counsel so that in every way the lord may be safeguarded as to person, rights, and belongings. The lord, similarly, has a reciprocal duty towards his faithful man. If either defaults in what he owes the other, he may justly be accused of perfidy. The language, of course, is that of an eminent school-

[2] *Ibid.*, p. 5.
[3] *Ibid.*, p. 23.

man with a taste for classical study. For "vassal" and "fief" he wrote *fidelis* and *beneficium*. And to expound the vassal's obligations he composed a sort of philosophical exercise. His information, nevertheless, is welcome; for the official documents of the eleventh and twelfth centuries describe the technicalities of fief-holding rather than the traditional ideals of vassalage.

How influential these ideals remained in feudal society is eloquently shown by the vernacular poetry of mediaeval France. Almost invariably the action in the *chansons de geste* turns upon the mutual faith of lord and vassal or, conversely, upon the failure of one to do all that he should for the other. Thus in the *Song of Roland*, the oldest and finest of the French epics, the rear-guard of Charlemagne's army is exposed to Saracen attack through the treachery of Ganelon. Roland, the hero, is the personification of courage and loyalty. Refusing to summon help by sounding his horn, he urges the French knights to charge the enemy without considering the odds against them. To his friend Oliver he declares that they must have only one thought, to fight to the death on behalf of their emperor.[4]

---

[4] Stanza LXXXVIII; cf. LXXIX.

For his lord man should suffer great hardships, should endure extremes of heat and cold, should lose his blood and his flesh. Strike with thy lance! And I will strike with Durendal, my good sword which the king gave me. If I die, may he who has it be able to say that it belonged to a noble vassal!

Vassalage, indeed, is the theme of the entire poem. The word is repeated time and again, and always to imply everything that a true knight ought to be—whatever, as will be seen in the next chapter, was embraced by the original code of chivalry. Who can read this glorious *chanson* without finding that its spirit carries him back to the Germanic custom pictured by Tacitus?

Ignoring for the moment all possible exceptions, we may say that a vassal was pre-eminently a gentleman and a warrior, pledged as such to support his lord on the battlefield and in other honorable ways. This was a personal obligation which feudal tenure could modify but never set aside. The fact that, by the eleventh century, a vassal normally lived on his own estate meant only that his attendance upon his lord was restricted to particular occasions—when, thanks to his enhanced position, his service would be especially valuable. Nor did the concession of a fief relieve the lord of personal responsibility towards his vassal. The faithless lord, as well as the faithless vassal, was known as a felon, and felony of one sort or another remained prominent in all systems of feudal law. Before pursuing that subject, however, we must know something more about the acquisition and tenure of fiefs.

In mediaeval France a fief was sharply distinguished from allodial property. The latter a *Inheritance of fiefs* man really owned, by virtue of an absolute title secured through inheritance, gift, or purchase. The former, on the contrary, a man held of some one else, enjoying at most what lawyers called the usufruct—a right to possession under certain conditions. To take a simple case, let us suppose that A gives the land of X to be held of him by his vassal E in return for specified service agreed on between the two. E's possession continues indefinitely, as long as he proves himself a faithful vassal and performs his owed service. When A is succeeded by a son B, E likewise becomes his vassal by rendering him homage. Even if, as was anciently possible, E could easily terminate his vassalage, he would not wish to do so; for he would then have to give up his fief, and he wants his son F to hold X on the same terms. That is agreeable to B, whose interest in maintaining a good vassal remains unchanged. But on E's death

F cannot legally obtain his father's fief until he in turn has rendered homage to B. Thereupon he receives investiture: the lord hands him a stick, a turf, a knife, or some other symbolic object to mark his formal possession of the fief.

In actual practice we know that, even before the close of the ninth century, it was customary for fiefs to pass from father to son; and that, within another hundred years or so, a fief was regularly described as hereditary. For reasons stated above, however, such inheritance is found to have been merely the renewal of a feudal contract, to which each of the parties, the lord and the vassal, had to give personal assent. When a vassal died, his fief reverted to the lord and really ceased to be a fief at all until another vassal had been invested with it. In case the vassal had no heir, the reversion was called escheat, and the lord was free to keep the dead man's estate or to regrant it to whomsoever he pleased. In case the vassal had an heir, the lord was legally obliged to accept him as the new holder. Yet even then a regrant was necessary through formal investiture; and in recognition of this fact the heir very commonly paid the lord a sum of money called relief.

Another striking peculiarity of feudal tenure

was primogeniture, the rule that a fief should pass intact to the eldest son. No such form of inheritance was known either to Roman or to Germanic law, and allodial property continued to be shared by the children of a deceased owner. The fact that a fief was legally indivisible seems to prove that it was considered a public office rather than a piece of land. This was obviously true in the case of a duchy or county. But it was no less true, at least originally, in the case of an ordinary fief, where the income from agrarian estates combined with a territorial immunity provided remuneration for the service, military and political, of a vassal. It was greatly to the interest of a princely donor that responsibility for the needed service should be concentrated. To allow a fief to be indefinitely partitioned would nullify its value—would, in fact, contravene the very purpose of its establishment. On the other hand, the recipient of a fief might well be permitted to assign parts of it to his own vassals, for their default would remain his liability. Primogeniture thus came to be adopted as a very practical regulation for the continuance of feudal tenure, and with the latter spread widely throughout mediaeval Europe. The only significant modification of the rule for the benefit of

Primo-geniture

younger children was the custom called parage.
Under it a fief could be divided among a number
of co-heirs if one of them rendered homage for
all of it and so in a way guaranteed its integrity.

*Ward-
ship and
marriage*

To introduce the subject of feudal inheritance
it has been necessary to re-emphasize the fact
that vassalage was always personal. A related fact
also had important consequences—that vassalage
was properly restricted to fighting-men. When
a vassal died leaving an infant son as heir, the
lord commonly enjoyed the right of wardship.
That is to say, he took the fief into his own
hands and, enjoying its revenue, supported the
heir until such time as the latter attained major-
ity. Then the youth, having been knighted and
declared of age, performed homage to the lord
and from him received investiture. This procedure logically solved the problem of a minority.
But suppose the holder of a fief had only a
daughter. If a girl could not be a vassal, how
could she be recognized as an heiress? The answer, of course, was provided by the institution
of marriage: a husband could render the necessary homage and acquire legal possession of the
fief. Such a marriage required the lord's consent
even during the lifetime of the girl's father.
When he was dead, the lord as guardian took

complete charge of the matter and, very generally, awarded the lady's hand to the noble suitor
who bid the highest. True, the relatives of a
young heir or heiress often objected to the lord's
pretensions, and he was sometimes compelled to
recognize one of them as guardian—on condition, however, that the latter became the lord's
vassal for the duration of the minority.

Thus, by a series of legal devices, it was ar-
ranged that a fief should pass from one mature *Military*
man to another; for the holder was normally re- *service*
quired to perform military service. Although detailed records of the service actually rendered
date only from the later Middle Ages, we may
be sure that the principles then set forth were
much older. Since at least the ninth century vassalage had implied a personal obligation to fight
for the lord as a heavy-armed cavalryman, or
knight.[5] But, in addition, a royal vassal who had
received a valuable fief was expected to bring
with him a mounted troop of his own vassals, and
the same requirement would apply to most men
who held of a duke, a count, or some other mag-
nate. It was in this way that the army of every
feudal prince was regularly made up. At first,
apparently, the size of each vassal's contingent

[5] See below, pp. 4cf.

and the length of his service were not precisely
determined in advance. By the twelfth century,
however, such determination had become usual
in the better-organized states, especially those
controlled by the Normans. According to the
perfected scheme, the vassal took with him into
the field enough knights to complete whatever
quota was charged against his fief, but he was
obliged to furnish the service at his own cost for
no more than forty days once in the year.

Subin-
feudation

To illustrate the working of feudal arrangements, we may take the following example,
though it should be remembered that so exact
a system was by no means universal. After con-
quering England, we shall suppose, William of
Normandy gives A, his vassal, twenty-five manors as a fief to be held for the service of ten
knights. A then has a choice of procedures. He
may, to use the technical phrases, keep all twenty-
five manors in demesne or he may subinfeudate
some of them to meet any part of his owed service. In the first case he will take from each manor
whatever is there produced through the labor
of the attached peasants and, when summoned to
the royal army, will have to induce nine other
knights to accompany him. The nine may be
vassals whom, according to ancient fashion, he

maintains in his household, or they may be knights whom he is able to hire. But, let us say, he finds it difficult to keep these men under his own roof and he lacks the cash for paying wages; he therefore adopts the alternate plan. He grants a fief of eight manors to his cousin (B), who promises him the service of four knights. And five landless adventurers (C, D, E, F, G) agree to become his vassals in return for one good manor each. The service due from A's fief is now provided for. In response to the king's summons A will go himself, together with his six vassals (B, C, D, E, F, G) and the three additional knights furnished by B. A, it will be noted, still has twelve manors in demesne, from which to support himself and his family. B, to take care of his owed service, has the same choice that A originally had. C, D, E, F, and G live on their respective manors and serve A in person. No matter how many stages of subinfeudation there may be, all are made possible by a pre-existing manorial organization.

That heavy expense was entailed by military service of this kind is apparent from the fact that *Aid and* it involved the finding, not only of trained men, *hospi-* but also of very superior horses, costly equip- *tality* ment, numerous servants, and enough food to supply the whole troop throughout the campaign. And the vassal's responsibility was by no means restricted to military service. On certain occasions he was required to pay his lord a contribution called aid. The northern French custom, taken by the Normans to England, specified three such occasions: the knighting of the lord's eldest son, the marriage of the lord's eldest daughter, and ransom of the lord when captured. In many regions, however, an aid could be exacted for the knighting of any son or the marriage of any daughter, and sometimes, as well, for a crusade, a journey to the royal court, or some other extraordinary undertaking. The vassal, furthermore, owed his lord hospitality. That is to say, whenever the lord came for a visit, the vassal was expected to provide free entertainment. And since every great lord was constantly moving about with a small army of mounted attendants, one could not afford to be too generous a host. As a consequence, the vassal's obligation in this respect often came to be strictly defined and was sometimes commuted into a money payment.

Suit to court

Every vassal, finally, was responsible for the important service called suit to court. When summoned to attend his lord, the vassal had to go in person and at his own expense. The reasons for the service were as varied as the meanings of the word "court." The occasion might be largely ceremonial, as in the case of a festival or the celebration of a wedding. Perhaps the lord wished to consult his men with regard to a war or a treaty. Very frequently they were asked to approve some act of government or to take part in a trial. For example, if the lord needed military service or financial aid beyond what was specifically owed by his vassals, his only recourse was to ask them for a voluntary grant. He had no right to tax or assess them arbitrarily, for his authority in such matters was determined by feudal contract. Nor did he have a discretionary power of legislation. Law was the unwritten custom of the country. To change or even to define it was the function, not of the lord, but of his court. It was the vassals themselves who declared the law under which they lived; and when one of them was accused of a misdeed, he was entitled to the judgment of his peers, i. e., his fellow vassals.

We are thus introduced to the subject of feudal justice, concerning which there has been much dispute. The phrase itself has often been the cause of disagreement. By feudal justice do we mean all the judicial rights enjoyed by a lord as *Feudal and seignorial justice* part of his fief, or only those exercised over men who held fiefs of him? Either usage is defensible, but to avoid ambiguity we may adopt the latter and apply the adjective "seignorial" to justice administered over non-vassals as well as vassals. Feudal justice can then be understood as merely one aspect of seignorial justice, and this understanding helps us to explain the development of both. Charlemagne's capitularies definitely prove that vassals, no matter what lords they had, remained subject to the jurisdiction of the public courts. So it is now generally held that a lord obtained the right to administer justice, not through his personal control over vassals, but through his acquisition of a fief. And for reasons already noted the fief brought him political authority only because it constituted a territorial immunity. In other words, seignorial government originated as a delegation of power by the monarchy and retained its essential character even under the enormously extended system of feudal tenures.

Although the variety of fiefs in eleventh-century France is at first glance bewildering, they resembled one another in being to some extent units of judicial, military, and fiscal administration. The simple knight, being a vassal at the bottom of the scale, would enjoy little more than the petty rights pertaining to a manorial court. On the other hand, the greater lord whose fief ranked as a barony [6] would have authority over a large number of people, including feudal tenants as well as rustics, both free and servile. When such a lord chose to raise a subsidy, he merely ordered an assessment of the non-noble population; but his vassals, as we have seen, could not be forced to contribute unless the occasion was one on which aid could lawfully be demanded of them. For the defense of his territory, likewise, the lord could require his vassals to perform only whatever service they owed for their fiefs, while ordinary men of the countryside might have to dig ditches, repair fortifications, cart supplies, or fight on foot with inferior weapons. What we call feudal justice was a similar differentiation for the benefit of the military class. From the system of judicial extortion that bore so heavily on the defenseless peasantry the vassal was exempt; his law was that declared by a truly feudal court, one made up of his peers.

The highly complicated subject of feudal law must here be passed over, except for brief mention of two characteristic features: trial by battle

Feudal trials

---

[6] See below, p. 60, n. 1.

and condemnation for felony. In any important case—as, for instance, a disputed claim to land or an accusation of unjustifiable homicide—a feudal court normally left the issue to be determined by judicial combat between the principals or their legally appointed champions. Then, in full knightly array, the two fought it out and the vanquished, if still alive, suffered whatever penalty the law prescribed.[7] Very generally any action unbefitting a feudal gentleman might be called felonious; more technically, however, felony was the disloyal refusal of a vassal to perform his owed service. If, for example, he absented himself from his lord's army and repeatedly ignored a consequent summons to his lord's court, this court could declare that, as a felon, he had forfeited his fief. But to such theoretical forfeiture a powerful vassal might well reply with a formal act of defiance (*diffidatio*) —the renunciation of fealty towards the lord on the ground that the latter had first broken faith with him. The result would of course be war, which to contemporaries was an extra-legal rather than an illegal mode of procedure.

---

[7] A very early and very graphic illustration is provided by the *Song of Roland* (CCLXXI–CCLXXXIX)—the duel between Thierry and Pinabel to decide the fate of Ganelon.

The foregoing discussion has dealt only with the standard form of feudal tenure. Under it fiefs held of a lord would bring him the following income, tangible or intangible: (1) homage and fealty; (2) knight service; (3) feudal aids; (4) entertainment; (5) suit to his court and the resulting profits of justice; (6) the so-called feudal incidents, which included relief, wardship, marriage, escheat, and forfeiture. But other forms of feudal tenure were not uncommon. From an early time castle-guard must have been the peculiar responsibility of certain fiefs. Instead of providing knights in the usual way, they sent contingents to a particular castle for a definite period in each year, so that among them a permanent garrison was maintained. Also, by a variety of tenure known to the English law as serjeanty, feudal contracts often required service other than that of knights. A fief might thus be made to furnish auxiliary troops, horses, arms, or other useful objects; members of a princely household might receive fiefs in return for the performance of their official duties. Finally, through the establishment of an alleged tenure in free alms, a church might be endowed with a fief that owed merely the service of prayer. Such a tenure, however, was hardly more than

Secondary forms of feudal tenure

a legal fiction and was by no means the universal privilege of ecclesiastics.

In this last connection a very pertinent question may already have been suggested to the reader: how from an early time vassalage, an essentially military relationship, could be assumed by so many clergymen, who were legally forbidden to take life or to shed blood. The answer is really quite simple. Throughout the ninth and tenth centuries such prohibition by the canon law, in spite of occasional protest, was generally ignored. Bishops, abbots, and other ecclesiastics not only acquired fiefs and performed homage but also fought like other vassals. The *Song of Roland* glorified an ancient tradition by having Archbishop Turpin die a hero's death on the field of battle. By the time that poem was written, however, the reinvigorated papacy had launched an ardent campaign to free the church of secular control. And although the idealistic program of the reformers could not be wholly carried out, they compelled the reluctant princes to accept important modifications of feudal practice.

The violent dispute over lay investiture thus resulted in a compromise by which feudal lords kept the right of investing ecclesiastics with fiefs

Clerical vassalage and fief-holding

and surrendered to the church merely the right of investing them with the symbols of holy office. In some countries, notably England and Normandy, the newly elected prelate still had to perform homage for his fief, "saving the rights of his order"; elsewhere a special arrangement permitted him merely to swear fealty. On all sides the rule was now generally enforced that a clergyman should personally abstain from warfare; whatever military service was due from his lay fief could be provided through subinfeudation. Like other vassals, he continued to owe the customary aids, hospitality, and suit to court, although he came to be excused from any judgment involving the death penalty or maiming. So, with only a few practical readjustments, feudal tenure retained its usefulness for all parties concerned. From a fief held by an ecclesiastical vassal the lord obtained very much the same service as from one held by a layman. The chief difference between the two was that the former produced no incidental revenue by way of relief, wardship, or marriage; but, to make up for that loss, the lord commonly took the income of such a fief during the interval between the death of a prelate and the installation of his successor.

One further modification of early feudal custom will serve to conclude the present discussion and, in a way, to introduce that which follows. Originally, we have every reason to believe, a man's vassalage was supposed to be exclusive. Even if a vassal could divide his loyalty between two lords, how could he simultaneously live in two households or follow two leaders in battle? It was obviously the practice of granting fiefs to vassals that relieved them of constant attendance upon the lord, permitted their service to be strictly defined, and, often enough, caused vassalage to be regarded as little more than a legal formality. As the older forms of proprietary grant were rapidly superseded by feudal tenure, it became virtually impossible to acquire wealth except by accumulating fiefs, and this compelled a fortunate recipient to be the vassal of numerous grantors. The logical consequence was the appearance by the twelfth century of a distinction between liege homage and ordinary homage. The former was rendered only to the principal lord and established the vassal's paramount obligations; the latter, as a mere prerequisite for fief-holding, could be repeated for any number of lords. Accordingly, despite the growing complexity of political and economic relationships, much of the original vassalage persisted well into the later Middle Ages. As long, indeed, as society continued to be dominated by the old warrior class, its traditional institutions, among them vassalage, retained their vigor. The truth of this statement will be better appreciated when we come to examine the system of belief and conduct that is called chivalry.

Chapter Three

CHIVALRY

Knight-hood and chivalry

Fʀᴏᴍ the preceding chapter it should be apparent that the typical member of the feudal aristocracy was at the same time a lord and a vassal. These next two chapters are intended to show how, in addition, he would normally be a knight and a nobleman. Whatever may have been the earlier meaning of the English word "knight" (Anglo-Saxon *cniht*), it came to be used after the Norman Conquest as the equivalent of the French *chevalier*. One might therefore think that "knighthood" and *chevalerie* would be synonymous terms, and so they are to the extent that both signify the status of knight. The French word, however, has a broader connotation; it may refer to the habits and ideals of the whole knightly order, and on that account has been introduced into our language as "chivalry."

Today, when we call a man chivalrous, we are

evidently thinking of a moral quality rather than a horse. But the fact remains, and it is an important one in the social history of Europe, that without a *cheval* nobody could be a *chevalier*. From the military point of view this matter of the horse is by no means so simple as it might at first appear. To obtain cavalry (*caballarii*) the mediaeval prince had to do more than put men on horses (*caballi*); he had, in particular, to consider the strength of the mounts together with the training and equipment of the riders. What kind of horses were then available? As late as 1066 we know that the Anglo-Saxons fought on foot; even the thegns who rode to the battlefield dismounted when they reached it. The reason, apparently, was that the native breed of horse was at best a sort of pony, useful merely for brief transportation. The troops of King Harold had no such chargers as bore the mailed knights of Duke William. And yet the horse of pre-Norman England was a valuable animal—so valuable that in tenth-century London one of the better grade was officially rated at four oxen, six cows, twelve pigs, or twenty-four sheep.[1]

Mediaeval horses

---

[1] See the doom (vi Aethelstan, 6), which provides the following indemnities for the theft of livestock: a horse, half a pound (120*d.*); an ox, 30*d.*; a cow, 20*d.*; a pig, 10*d.*; a sheep, 5*d.*

Since the maximum possession of the ordinary peasant was a yoke of oxen, only a quite superior person was expected to ride a horse at all. How much greater the distinction in being a twelfth-century knight, whose *destrier* [2] might well be worth several hundred sheep!

Knight service and its social significance

The early Franks seem to have fought on foot like the Anglo-Saxons, and for the same reason. By the middle of the ninth century, on the contrary, the typical Frankish soldier had come to fight on horseback, being equipped for that purpose with shirt of mail, helmet, shield, lance, and sword. Although the subject remains very obscure for lack of investigation, the new military system was probably learned from the Byzantine Empire, where the use of heavy-armed cavalry (*cataphracti*) [3]—as distinguished from the light cavalry of the Huns, Goths, and other barbarians —had been perfected long before the reign of Charlemagne. However introduced, the employment of such troops in the west, as in the east, must have been made possible by the improved

Translated in F. L. Attenborough, *The Laws of the Earliest English Kings* (Cambridge, 1922), p. 161.

[2] Latin *dextrarius;* so called, it is said, because the right hand was used for leading the horse.

[3] On the use of these troops and the related problem of the war-horse see W. W. Tarn, *Hellenistic Military and Naval Developments* (Cambridge, 1930), pp. 73 f.

breed of war-horses which, our best authorities declare, was first developed across the Roman frontier in Asia. We may also be sure that a great horse of this kind was far beyond the means of the average Frank; [4] and that, even if the king found him a mount and the appropriate equipment, he could hardly know what to do with them. So it happened that the Carolingians, desiring trained cavalry and lacking funds wherewith to hire mercenaries, adopted the expedient of granting fiefs to their vassals on condition that they would furnish the needed service.

At least in the western Frankish kingdom the military revolution thus begun had been completed by the opening of the tenth century. Thenceforward the Latin records of France use *miles*, the classic word for the Roman legionary, as the perfect equivalent of *chevalier*. The man who fought on foot came to be disregarded; he could be no more than a miserable rustic, poorly armed, ill disciplined, and spiritless. The only true soldier was the feudal gentleman, the mem-

---

[4] A Frankish compilation of the early eighth century, the *Law of the Ripuarian Franks* (xxxvi, 11), gives the following valuations: a horse, 12s.; a shirt of mail, 12s.; a sword with a sheath, 7s.; a helmet, 6s.; leggings, 6s.; a shield and a lance, 2s. The total is 45s. which, according to the same source, was the equivalent of more than twenty-two oxen. These laws have not been translated into English.

ber of an aristocratic family whose wealth provided not only the material equipment but also the leisure for a knightly upbringing. The gulf between the warrior class and the peasant class had never been easy to cross; it now became virtually impassable. In the time of Charlemagne we hear of serfs "honored with vassalage" so that they had horses and bore arms. Similarly, in the later Middle Ages, various princely courts included *ministeriales*—servile retainers who, thanks to their lord's patronage, acquired estates and lived like barons. But such cases were always exceptional and the taint of base blood was not soon forgotten. More significant is the fact that a plowman's son, however free in person, could not hope to enter the military profession, simply because he had no chance of obtaining a chivalrous education.

Chivalrous education

Perhaps the best way to explain knighthood is to compare it with other professional attainments. To become a priest, the youth had to reach a mature age, acquire a certain proficiency in Latin letters, and otherwise demonstrate his fitness for holy office; then he was solemnly ordained by a bishop. So too, in any craft, no one could become a master without serving his apprenticeship and passing numerous tests. And in the later university a degree was conferred on a candidate only after he had successfully prepared himself by years of specialized study. A person could no more be born a knight than he could be born a priest, a master of a gild, or a doctor of medicine. It was necessary for him to earn the rank through long and arduous training. This training began in infancy. The boy of aristocratic family, except possibly when destined for the church, would be set to learning horsemanship and the use of arms almost as soon as he could walk. Very often, at the age of seven or eight, he would be sent away from home to be brought up at the court of his father's lord or of some distinguished relative. There he would be expected not only to develop skill in all martial exercises but also to become familiar with the ways of life in and about the halls of the great. Though never treated as a menial, he would have to make himself useful in a variety of tasks, from running errands for ladies to assisting knights with their horses and harness. And many of his most valuable lessons, like those of a modern schoolboy, would be learned in the rough game of give and take with his fellows.

Throughout the whole term of his apprenticeship in arms the youth was commonly known

in French as a *valet* or *damoiseau*—i. e., a little
vassal or a little lord; for the first word is derived
from the diminutive of *vassalus*, the second from
that of *dominus*. Sometimes, particularly in England, he was called a page during his younger
years. In any case, when he reached the age of
about fourteen, he acquired a new title, that of
squire (French *écuyer*, or shield-bearer). Henceforth he was regularly attached to an individual
knight, whom it was his duty to accompany and
assist. In the event of battle, the squire carried
the knight's reserve of arms, led his extra horse
if he had one, laced on his defensive armor,
rescued him when dismounted or wounded, and
took charge of any prisoners he might capture.
Through such activity the squire learned the
brutal business of war at first hand. Meanwhile,
as he grew in size and strength, he became more
adept in the use of a man's weapons, as in fencing
with a sword and tilting with a lance. Squires
fought sham battles with one another or charged
at a quintain, a dummy or other target set on a
post in such a way as to test the rider's skill in
striking it fairly with his lance. Finally, when the
squire had proved himself a true warrior, especially by his conduct in actual battle, he was
rewarded with knighthood.

Tacitus, it will be remembered, describes the ancient German custom by which a youth was presented with a shield and a spear to mark his attainment of man's estate. What seems to be the same ceremony reappears under the Carolingians. In 791, we are told, Charlemagne caused Prince Louis to be girded with a sword in celebration of his adolescence; and forty-seven years later Louis in turn decorated his fifteen-year-old son Charles "with the arms of manhood, i. e., a sword." Here, obviously, we may see the origin of the later *adoubement*, which long remained a formal investiture with arms, or with some one of them as a symbol. Thus the Bayeux Tapestry represents the knighting of Earl Harold by William of Normandy under the legend: *Hic Willelmus dedit Haroldo arma* (Here William gave arms to Harold). The earl, already dressed in armor, holds a lance in his left hand and with his right has apparently just placed a sword at his waist; the duke completes the armament by putting a helmet on his head.[5] Scores of other examples are to be found in the French chronicles and *chansons de geste* which, despite much variation of detail, agree on the essentials. And whatever the derivation of the words, the English ex-

Adoubement

---

[5] See Figure 1 (from the Bayeux Tapestry) and below, p. 61.

pression "dubbing to knighthood" must have been closely related to the French *adoubement*. A Latin historian states that Henry, son of William the Conqueror, "assumed arms by gift of

FIGURE 1.—WILLIAM KNIGHTS HAROLD

his father" (*sumpsit arma a patre*), while the Anglo-Saxon Chronicle reports that the king *dubbade his sunu Henric to ridere*.[6] In the feudal age, to be sure, *adoubement* was usually postponed until a youth was twenty or twenty-one;

---

[6] I. e., rider or knight; cf. the German *ritter*.

but the postponement clearly resulted from the increasing difficulty of learning the military profession, combined with the need of greater maturity on the part of a prospective fief-holder.

Although any knight could thus create a knight, the honor, like that described by Tacitus, was usually conferred by the boy's father, another of his relatives, or one of the chief men in the locality; and it was the more highly prized when received at the hands of a distinguished warrior. Especially proud was the squire whose bravery was summarily rewarded on the field of battle. In that case the ceremony would undoubtedly retain its ancient simplicity, including at most the presentation of a sword, a few words of admonition, and the accolade. This last was originally no polite tap, but a sturdy blow delivered on the nape of the neck (French *col*)— evidently the traditional means of impressing upon the youth the solemnity of his new engagement. These elements were still prominent in the great festivals which celebrated the knighting of a king's son or other prince in the twelfth century, and which, as we have seen, often occasioned the levy of a feudal aid. In such a courtly atmosphere, however, the *adoubement* was preceded by an elaborate ritual and followed by an exhibition of skill on the part of the initiate and his high-born companions.

Of the many formulas that might be spoken while delivering the accolade, the most eloquent was also the briefest: *Sois preux!* To be *preux* was to conduct oneself as a true knight; nothing more had to be said. But for the modern reader, who lacks a chivalrous education, the word has lost its force. "Prowess" (*prouesse*) can mean to him only a vague accomplishment of some sort. In order to regain the understanding of the feudal age he must study examples, and of these the finest is Roland, whose glory was approached by no other character of mediaeval epic. The qualities pre-eminently displayed by that great hero are quite unmistakable. First of all, Roland is brave—brave to the point of absolute recklessness. He and the best part of Charlemagne's army are slain because he scorns the advice of Oliver; he will not sound his horn until no more can be gained than revenge for his death. "Oliver," declares the poet, "is sensible; Roland is *preux.*" Gallantly he charges straight against the enemy, expressing the proud hope that, should he fall, he may be remembered as a "noble vassal." Roland, the *chanson* tells us, is betrothed to

Aude and we are allowed to guess that he cher-
ishes her as he should. For Oliver, his companion-
in-arms, Roland has deep affection. And he is
always a devoted son of the church. It is not,
however, love or friendship or religion that
makes Roland's conduct heroic; it is vassalage.
At the critical moment his loyalty is undivided;
in simple faith to his lord he blithely offers up
everything he has.

From the *Song of Roland*, as well as from
many other sources, we may conclude that the
ancient virtues of the barbarian warrior remained
fundamental to the chivalry of the eleventh century. Prowess, above all else, implied valor and
fidelity. No gentleman could afford to incur the
merest suspicion of cowardice or treachery. Because it was braver to attack boldly, the true
knight disdained all tricks in combat; he would
not strike an unarmed or unprepared foe. His
pledge of faith must be kept at all costs. The
knight who yielded himself to another would
never attempt to escape; he could regain his
freedom only through rescue by a friend or payment of ransom. But loyalty to the plighted
word, it should be remembered, was only one
side of a mutual obligation. The honor that
bound a knightly prisoner was supposed to be

respected by honorable treatment on the part of his captor. A faithful vassal must be deserved by a faithful lord. To brook insult and neglect was no duty of the chivalrous; the proper reply to any sort of injury was formal defiance. Proud gentlemen were quick to take offense and plunge their families in the bloody feuds so often depicted by the chronicles and *chansons de geste*. In such action contemporaries saw no violation of the knightly code.

The etiquette of chivalry

Every society tends to have a system of etiquette, which is obeyed much more scrupulously than the dictates of positive law—think merely of what a respectable man will and will not do today. So it was in the Middle Ages. The etiquette of chivalry was recognized wherever feudal institutions prevailed because it spelled honor to the feudal aristocracy. In opposition to this statement it may be said that mediaeval writings describe all sorts of atrocities committed by men of the highest birth. But whose opinion are we to consider? Latin histories, being written for learned ecclesiastics, might condemn much that seemed innocent to ordinary laymen. The views of the latter are rather to be found in the *chansons de geste*, which were written in the vernacular to please an aristocratic audience. If we take for granted that no such work would approve anything that most knights considered disgraceful, we may draw some interesting conclusions. Gallant gentlemen, it would appear, had no antipathy to violence and cruelty; within the accepted rules of combat they were expected to be bloodthirsty and ruthless. And whatever courtesy they displayed was reserved for members of their own order. For a knight to live by war and rapine, pillaging churches and slaughtering peasants on the lands of an enemy, was quite normal. Women he properly regarded as at most a valuable commodity. A wife's duty was to rear children and maintain domestic peace; one who talked too much earned a slap in the face. The modern reader who is shocked by the conduct of the hero in a feudal epic has failed to understand the primitive chivalry—to realize that it implied no more than the respect of one warrior for another.

Chivalry, therefore, was originally non-Christian. But as the purified church extended its influence over all phases of life in the twelfth century, chivalry acquired at least a tinge of religion. Clerical participation in the ceremony of *adoubement* seems to have begun with the blessing of the arms given to the initiate. Logically, then, the

Religious and literary influences

latter might be required to prepare himself for the honor by fasting, prayer, and attendance at mass; before receiving the accolade he might hear a sermon on the duties of the Christian soldier. In the great pageants that celebrated the knighting of princes such ecclesiastical features became especially prominent. Yet no one of them was ever essential to *adoubement*, and that any of them seriously affected the chivalrous tradition may well be doubted. Generation after generation, the aristocracy gave little heed to the preachers who denounced fighting for the sake of glory and booty as sheer murder and robbery. And who, aside from pious schoolmen, read the books that explained knighthood in terms of Christian symbolism? To secure the unqualified service of a knight the church had to enroll him in one of the crusading orders—and that made him into a sort of monk instead of a feudal gentleman.

The chivalry with which we are here concerned was no structure of the clerical imagination; nor was it a story-teller's fancy. As long as the society of western Europe was dominated by the knightly class—a class whose traditions were essentially those of the barbarian warrior—chivalry continued to be a very real institution.

It was already old when the first *chansons de geste* were written; they merely accepted and somewhat idealized it. For the ingrained habits and prejudices of most knights defied all literary influence, whether religious or secular. Throughout the twelfth century the original chivalry seems on the whole to have persisted. The growing luxury of the age, to be sure, encouraged new standards of politeness, which were largely dictated by women. At least in a few princely courts romantic poetry attained great vogue. Fine gentlemen now composed lyrics in honor of their ladies and sighed over tales of love and adventure in far-off lands. But we can hardly escape the feeling that the new fashion was little more than affectation. The average knight, we must believe, went about his business of warfare in the same old way, untroubled by the thought that, to be truly chivalrous, he must be chronically amorous.

Chapter Four

THE FEUDAL NOBILITY

TIME and again in the preceding pages we have had occasion to remark that the feudal age was intensely aristocratic. The ruling class was made up of fief-holders who, as such, enjoyed a virtual monopoly of wealth, of military prestige, and of political authority. A member of this class was necessarily the vassal of the lord from whom he held his fief; with respect to his own tenants he was himself a lord; professionally, except in the case of a clergyman, he had to be a knight; by birth he ranked as a nobleman. Since the feudal nobility was thus composed of fief-holders and their families, it eventually became possible in some countries to acquire a noble title by the purchase of a noble estate. But this amounted to a reversal of the old law. Under the original feudalism nobility was a matter of personal status. Fief-holding, as we have seen, presupposed vassalage; and vassalage presupposed a warlike aristocracy. The Franks, both before and after their conquest of Gaul, were distinguished as a nation of fighting-men. To be a Frank in the fullest sense of the word—i. e., a man who was really "free"—one had to belong to the warrior class.

There is every reason to believe that, even in the Merovingian kingdom, the typical warrior was sharply distinguished from the typical peasant. The latter, although he might be legally free, was at most an economic dependant; the former, on the contrary, was to some extent a landed proprietor and was thus enabled to maintain the standard of a barbarian gentleman. He might, in fact, be officially styled *gentilis*, or perhaps *nobilis;* for the two expressions remained synonymous throughout the early Middle Ages. Yet, however superior he might be to the ordinary peasant, the primitive noble could hardly equip himself as a heavy-armed cavalryman. So the prince who wanted such service had to keep up an expensive household or, like the Carolingians, enrich his vassals with fiefs. The result, as explained above, was the rapid development of an exalted social order, the chivalrous class of the feudal age. And for hundreds of years the members of this class, together with their wives and children, constituted the nobility of Europe. To be a nobleman was thus to be a knight, or at least a candidate for knighthood; originally, if a youth of gentle birth abandoned the military profession, he abandoned also his rank in society. A woman, of course, enjoyed nothing in her own name; since she could not be a knight, she could expect no greater honor than to be married to one.

The feudal hierarchy

To appreciate the mediaeval concept of nobility, we must disregard such later creations as the British peerage. In our language the ancient tradition is better retained by "gentleman" than by "nobleman." There are no grades of gentility; a gentleman is a gentleman, without regard to wealth or political eminence. So it was in the case of a knight. To the extent that chivalry was the essence of nobility, a man's true worth could only be proved in battle. Except in the field, however, nobility was also a matter of feudal possessions. Most knights were vassals and as such had obtained fiefs. One who held a greater fief ranked as a greater vassal, and from that point of view as a greater noble. By the eleventh century the French had thus come to recognize a feudal hierarchy which, despite much variation of local usage, was generally distinguished by a

series of characteristic titles. Some of these titles
were of Carolingian, some of later, origin. By re-
viewing them we should learn something about
the composition of the noble class, as well as
something about its early development.

First of all, we have to consider the rulers of
the principalities, the great royal fiefs that had
become virtually independent. The model for
such a principality was the Carolingian march,
to constitute which a number of counties had
been placed under a military commander styled
marquis or duke. In the feudal age Normandy,
Burgundy, Aquitaine, and Gascony were commonly known as duchies, but other territories
of the same kind as counties. For example, the
old march of Gothia was called the county of
Toulouse after it had been acquired by the count
of that city; and similar usage prevailed in such
important states as Flanders and Champagne.
Sometimes, on the other hand, the title of count
retained its earlier force, being given to the head
of a small district included within a duchy. The
viscount, as the word implies, was at first a
count's deputy. By the eleventh century he had
sometimes, as in Aquitaine, made his office into a
fief; sometimes, as in Normandy, he remained
an administrative official appointed by the prince.

The main duty of the castellan or *châtelain* was
to keep one of his lord's castles—a vital function
in the defense of every large fief and one that,
for example in Flanders, might be associated with
other governmental powers. Although any vassal could properly be referred to as a baron [1] or
seigneur, those titles were often used technically
to distinguish noblemen of superior rank from
mere *chevaliers*. The former were said to possess
baronies or *seigneuries* and were expected to
have numerous vassals of their own, whereas the
latter would hold only enough property to permit knightly service in person.

Two additional titles that were sometimes
borne by French nobles resulted from the ecclesiastical reform of the eleventh century. Clergymen, as we have seen, had earlier taken active
part in warfare. Then, with the strict enforcement of the canon law, it became usual for local
churches to appoint lay protectors and to com-
pensate them by the grant of fiefs. In the case
of a monastery the appointee was called an *avoué*
(*advocatus*), in that of a bishopric a *vidame*
(*vicedominus*). And all too often, if we may believe the complaints preserved in legal records,
the hereditary possession of such an office by a

---

[1] From the late Latin *baro*, a man.

feudal house was turned into a pretext for robbery and extortion; the church had to appeal to the king for protection against its "protector." Meanwhile the exclusion of high-born prelates from the military profession had necessarily involved their exclusion from the chivalrous aristocracy. Yet, because they were great fief-holders, they continued to be recognized as great nobles; under the Capetian monarchy some of them came to enjoy the official rank of duke or count. The political significance of the nobility, however, is a subject that will be more fully treated in the following chapter; for the moment we may turn to such activities of everyday life as more directly interested the gentlemen of the feudal age.

The noble warrior of the eleventh century is most vividly depicted for us in the Bayeux Tapestry, a strip of linen with scenes worked in colored thread to describe the Norman Conquest of England. As there represented, a man's ordinary clothing consisted primarily of a loose tunic belted at the waist and, below it, tight-fitting hose. When peacefully engaged, he might also wear a cape or mantle, fastened by a clasp at the throat and sometimes provided with a hood that could be pulled over the head. In case

Arms and armor

of a warlike expedition the mantle was replaced by a hauberk, a shirt of mail that was constructed by sewing metal scales on a leather foundation

FIGURE 2.—HAROLD ABOUT TO RECEIVE THE CROWN

or—the much more expensive process—by welding iron links to form a continuous fabric. Such a hauberk reached only to the knee and was slashed at the bottom to enable the wearer to ride on horseback. It had elbow-length sleeves and a sort of hood that furnished a mailed covering for the back of the neck and, presumably, a padded lining for the helmet. The latter was a conical iron cap with a frontal extension over the nose. Otherwise the knight's face was left unprotected, as were his forearms and his lower legs, except for what would now be called put-

FIGURE 3.—ARMS ARE CARRIED TO THE NORMAN SHIPS

tees. Leggings of mail, according to the tapestry, were as yet the mark of a distinguished person, more particularly the Norman duke. For additional defense the knight carried a long kite-shaped shield by means of thongs attached to its under side. Its outer side, probably a metal facing on a wooden base, might be decorated with a picture or geometrical pattern.[2] For offense his customary weapons were a lance, about

---

[2] See the cover figure, which, like all the accompanying figures, is taken from the Bayeux Tapestry.

eight feet in length, and a cross-hilted sword, which was slung at his waist on the left side.

The charger

Like the contemporary feudal epic, the Bayeux Tapestry glorifies horses as well as knights. The anonymous artist seems to have delighted in

FIGURE 4.—A NORMAN KNIGHT AND HIS CHARGER

drawing the great stallions of the Norman array, together with the smallest details of their harness. We thus find accurate representations of bridles, reins, stirrups, and saddles—even of the girths and breast-straps by which the latter were bound on. The mediaeval saddle, we may note, was of oriental design, highly peaked in front and in back, and probably, like the charger that bore it, had been introduced from the east. Whatever their origin, saddle and stirrups were of prime importance to the knight. Dressed in cumbersome armor, with a shield on his left arm and the reins in his left hand, he was supposed to ride at a gallop and strike an enemy with the lance couched in his right hand while he warded off a similar attack directed against himself. How could he do all this unless he had a firm seat on his horse? Hastings, of course, was not a battle between mounted armies; but the Bayeux Tapestry gives a spirited portrayal of the Norman charge and shows how the knight, after hurling or breaking his lance, fell to with his sword at close quarters.

The twelfth century witnessed very little change in military costume. The main piece of armor continued to be the hauberk, now regularly of link mail and of somewhat improved design, to protect the forearms and the chin. For a tournament the knight occasionally donned a barrel-shaped helmet that entirely covered the face and had mere slits for eye-holes. But since equipment of this sort left him half-blind, he commonly preferred the old-fashioned helmet for active war. His weapons were still a lance and a sword—sometimes also a battle-axe, although the Bayeux Tapestry shows it used only by the English. Shields, too, remained very much the

Beginnings of heraldry

same, except that they tended to be smaller and came to bear recognized coats of arms. Such devices were not solely a matter of ornament. A knight was effectively disguised even by the more primitive armor; in a famous scene of the Bayeux Tapestry Duke William has to lift his helmet to disprove the rumor that he has fallen. So we may imagine that, as a design painted on a shield served to identify the owner, it might become a permanent feature of his accoutrement and eventually a mark of pride for his descendants. By the close of the twelfth century, at any rate, it was already customary for every great house to have a characteristic blazon—a peculiar armorial bearing for the chief, which could be modified indefinitely to distinguish his relatives and vassals. Familiar examples are the *fleurs de lys* of the Capetians and the leopards [3] of the Angevins.

Feudal warfare

The general character of feudal warfare may be easily deduced from what has already been said about vassalage and chivalry. Although the feudal army sometimes included archers or other foot-soldiers, it was essentially a force of knights.

---

[3] In heraldry the only difference between a leopard and a lion is that the former shows his full face, the latter his profile. The so-called lions of England are therefore leopards.

Every knight was a gentleman warrior, devoted above all else to a creed of personal gallantry, which was hardly compatible with military discipline. His bravery was that of a reckless adventurer. His loyalty was primarily that of a vassal to a particular lord. And even the perfect

FIGURE 5.—"HERE IS DUKE WILLIAM"

vassal was by no means blind to his own interest —especially to the profit that arose from the taking of booty and the holding of noble prisoners to ransom. Accordingly, when two feudal armies met, each knightly participant was apt to conduct himself very much as he saw fit. The final outcome would depend on a series of duels in which the determining factor was individual prowess. But battles on a large scale were rare in feudal Europe. The characteristic warfare of the age consisted rather of pillaging raids into the enemy's territory, of skirmishes between small bands of knights, and of engagements incident to the siege of castles.

The complicated subject of military architecture in the early Middle Ages must here be reduced to a brief outline. Our word "castle," like the French *château*, is derived from the Old French *castel* and so from the Latin *castellum*, diminutive of *castra*. In the late Roman Empire the *castra* was a legionary camp, permanently constructed of masonry to enclose about fifty acres, while the *castellum* was a little fort of perhaps a fifth that size. The barbarian conquerors, however, came to apply both Latin names, together with the German *burg*, to any fortified place, even a walled city; and this usage persisted into the subsequent period, when local rulers built a variety of new strongholds. Among the latter, if we look beyond the words to the things designated, we may distinguish two principal types. The more primitive, which is found in England as well as on the continent, was a rude imitation of the Roman *castra*—usually an area of about thirty acres surrounded by a ditch, an earthen embankment, and a wooden palisade. Although such a work might serve as headquar-

Early mediaeval fortification

ters for a prince or his official, it was primarily
designed as a refuge, to be manned by the people
of the neighborhood when threatened by Viking
or Hungarian attack. The other type of fortress
appears to have been a peculiarly French development of the tenth century. It was relatively small,
normally of less than six acres in extent, and was
characterized by internal division into two parts
called the motte and the bailey. This is what we
properly know as the feudal castle.

Once again the Bayeux Tapestry gives us valuable information. Through a somewhat conven- *The*
tionalized art we are shown how Duke William *motte-
and-bailey*
took the castles of Dol, Rennes, and Dinant; *castle*
stopped at the castle of Bayeux; and, on landing
in England, immediately ordered that a similar
castle "be dug" at Hastings. This last scene is
intended to represent the construction of a motte
—i. e., an artificial mound which, by artistic an-
ticipation, is already provided with a stockade.
The foregoing scenes furnish additional details
of the contemporary castle: notably the cleated
drawbridge that rose over the moat to a gate in
the stockade and, inside the latter, the high
wooden tower or keep. In each case the tapestry
leaves us to imagine a bailey, the extensive court-
yard which was likewise protected by a moat,

drawbridge, and stockade and which enclosed the indispensable barracks, stables, and barns. During an attack the bailey served as an advanced

FIGURE 6.—CONSTRUCTION OF A CASTLE AT HASTINGS

position whence, if necessary, the defenders could withdraw to the motte with its stronger line of fortifications and its central tower. That the main purpose of the keep was military needs no elaborate proof, but it also constituted the permanent residence of whatever lord commanded the castle. He and his family lived in the upper storeys, which were accordingly partitioned to form a great hall, a chapel, and a series of private chambers. Above, the roof or garret would be specially designed for observation and the hurling of missiles. Below, the first storey would house the arms that were kept in reserve and the soldiers who guarded the entrance. An underground basement would contain a well and rooms

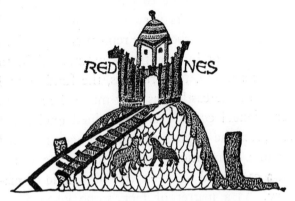

FIGURE 7.—THE CASTLE OF RENNES

for the storage of food, though cooking would normally be done in an outside kitchen.

The motte-and-bailey castle thus reflected its feudal origin. Although it might sometimes shelter a good many refugees, such a fortress was intended for continuous occupation by a military chieftain and a garrison of his vassals—that is to say, by professional warriors. Defenses of this type were thought so essential to feudal organization that the expansion of the latter can be accurately traced from the ruins of the former. The progress of the Normans in the British Isles, for example, was marked by the erection of no less than five hundred motte-and-bailey castles. There, as elsewhere, the individual plans varied somewhat from place to place. Wherever possible the conquerors very naturally saved time and labor by incorporating remnants of previous fortification or by adapting a natural height to serve as a motte. Nevertheless, the fundamental outline of the castle was very much the same in every feudal country and remained unchanged even after the original timber had been replaced by stone. Romantic fiction still fosters the notion that a castle had to be a tremendous pile of masonry. As a matter of fact, stone keeps were exceptional until the later twelfth century and the first to be raised were mere replicas of the old wooden structures—rectangular towers that stood apart from the encircling walls. A round keep or an integrated castle with rounded bastions can positively be attributed to the period after 1200.

Diver-sions of the feudal noble

By no means every feudal noble possessed a castle. Simple knights, the little vassals at the bottom of the scale, could expect to have no more than stockaded manor houses. Indeed, many a greater person lived in a similar way and even the most glorious princes spent a good portion of each year on their rural estates. The reason, of course, was not that they delighted in agrarian superintendence, but that much of their income consisted of produce which it was easier to consume than to transport. Under the traditional economy of the early Middle Ages agriculture was considered a necessary means of subsistence rather than a profitable business. The enforcement of its customary routine could well be left to local stewards or bailiffs. And so far as domestic management was concerned, what else did a wife have to occupy her time? The feudal gentleman, in other words, believed in maintaining the barbarian standard of gentility. His true vocation was fighting. Between campaigns he might for a time enjoy hunting, feasting, drinking, gambling, and love-making. Sooner or later, however, he became intensely bored with peace. Then he could do no better than ride to a tournament.

That favorite sport of the aristocracy was originally a battle in every sense of the word except that it was formally proclaimed and was fought according to particular rules agreed on in advance. Under the patronage of a chivalrous lord—and generous sponsors were never lacking—a day would be set for an encounter between two groups of knights, often representing two rival houses or localities. Dressed in full panoply of war, the contestants would align their mounts on either side of a field and then, at a given signal, charge. After lances had been broken, the combat would be continued with swords until one of the parties had been driven off or disarmed. Needless to say, it was a dangerous game in which blood was spilled and lives might be lost. But there was great honor to be won as well as booty; for a victor could claim the horse and arms of a vanquished opponent unless the latter ransomed them for a sum of money. A general affray of this sort, the tournament proper, was often accompanied by prearranged contests between pairs of knights; and with the passage of time such jousts, as they were called, became increasingly popular and increasingly showy. It was only at a much later time, however, that they degenerated into mere pageants. Men of the feudal age fought for the love of fighting, not—with blunted weapons—for love of the ladies.

Chapter Five

FEUDALISM AND THE MEDIAEVAL STATE

FEUDALISM, it is often asserted, was politically baneful in that it necessarily led to the disintegration of the state. But this opinion seems to have originated with historians who restricted their attention to the Carolingian Empire and the major kingdoms into which it was broken. Such large states, as we have seen, tended to die through internal weakness, not because their rulers tried to hold them together by means of feudal tenure. If we turn from them to the French duchies of the tenth and eleventh centuries, we gain a very different impression. In a little state, evidently, feudalism was not incompatible with efficient government, and the determining factor, we may suspect, was vassalage; for the strength of that personal bond, on which the whole feudal structure depended, was in-

The nature of the feudal state

evitably affected by local conditions. Experience proved only too well that trustworthy men might have untrustworthy sons, that to endow vassals with rich fiefs was to give them the means of successful revolt, and that the loyalty of distant officials could not be assured by compelling them to perform homage. According to ancient tradition, lord and vassal were bound together by mutual faith; if either proved false, the other was justified in renouncing the original agreement. So delicately balanced an obligation could have slight permanence unless it was of real advantage to both parties. When a lord was so weak or so far-removed that he could furnish no effective support to a vassal, the latter had every reason to defy his authority.

We may therefore conclude that the feudal state, one whose government largely depended on feudal tenure, had to be small because such tenure presupposed a close personal relationship between a lord and his vassals. But territorial extent is not the only matter to be taken into account; the political tradition of the countryside and the character of the ruling house might be of equal importance. To take a familiar example, let us consider the dominions of the Angevin Henry II, which in some fashion or another included the British Isles, Normandy, Aquitaine, Anjou, and Brittany. The last four he held as vassal of the French king. He was himself duke of Normandy, duke of Aquitaine, and count of Anjou; the county of Brittany was held of him by his son Geoffrey. Henry, of course, was king of England in his own right. In addition he was recognized as lord by various Irish chiefs and Welsh princes, by the Normans who had conquered parts of Ireland and Wales, and by the king of the Scots. Though often misnamed Angevin Empire, this collection of lands had little unity. Even the general acceptance throughout them of feudal custom was practically meaningless; for we cannot deduce Henry's actual power in a particular region from the fact that he held it as a fief rather than in full sovereignty, or from the fact that it was held of him by a vassal. In each case we have to know what rights were customarily enjoyed by the parties to the contract and in what measure those rights continued to be enforced. To understand how feudalism really worked, we must turn to the history of individual countries.

So far as eleventh-century France is concerned, we may disregard the royal authority *France* altogether. The kingdom of the West Franks, which had never been more than a political make-shift, now seemed on the point of final dissolution. The glorious reconstruction of the monarchy by the later Capetians could not possibly be foreseen. On the contrary, the disgraceful reign of Philip I (1060–1108) served to erase the little honor that yet clung to the kingly office. The ancient rights of the crown had long since passed to such men as were able, with or without legal authorization, to organize and defend a local territory. And although a territory of this sort might still be called a royal fief, the traditional language was generally belied by the conduct of the holder. The greater of the king's alleged vassals never came near his court, whether to perform homage or to render any other service. What respect could they have for a theoretical lord who was defied with impunity by petty officials on his own domain? France, obviously, had ceased to be a state in any proper sense of the word. Rather, it had been split into a number of states whose rulers, no matter how they styled themselves, enjoyed the substance of the regal power.

The early development of the French duchies remains very obscure through lack of contemporary records; yet we may be certain of at least a few important facts. It was typical of the age that three military commands set up by Charles the Bald for the defense of his northern frontiers should be turned into hereditary principalities. One of them we know as the county of Flanders, another as the duchy of Burgundy. The third was the march of Neustria, which became the royal domain when its rulers, beginning with Hugh Capet, obtained permanent title to the crown of France. By that time, however, their principality had been reduced to little more than the Île de France; for the counts of Anjou, Blois, and Champagne had made themselves virtually independent, and the Norman conquests along the Channel had been formally recognized as a separate duchy. The case of the last-named state is particularly interesting. The Viking invaders of the ninth century had assuredly been quite ignorant of feudal custom. If their descendants were able to construct a duchy that was based on such custom, it must have been by virtue of knowledge acquired in France. We should not suppose that the Norman dukes, for all their political genius, could have done more than improve on a French model; and this supposition

The French Duchies:

is borne out by the fact that their principality was not fundamentally different from the neighboring ones.

Flanders

In Flanders the Normans could find a particularly useful example. Whatever powers had earlier been wielded by the king had there fallen into the hands of the count. Of the numerous royal vassals who had once been scattered throughout the Flemish territory he alone was left. The others had transferred their allegiance to him, to serve as ministers of his household, as officials for local administration, as prelates of the church, or as knights in his army. The count, being thus the supreme military commander of Flanders, could muster for its defense all ablebodied inhabitants, as well as the mounted contingents owed by his feudal tenants. On every side important roads and waterways were dominated by his fortifications, to maintain which he had extensive rights of conscripting labor and requisitioning materials. No castle could be raised without his license or held in opposition to his orders. The count, furthermore, declared himself guardian of the general peace. Ordinary cases might be disposed of in the courts of his vassals, but his justice was paramount. All Flemish churches were under his special protection; only he could enjoy the *avouérie* [1] of monasteries. Within the economic sphere it was the count, or persons authorized by him, who coined money, regulated commerce, and levied indirect taxes. Precisely when and how he had come to exercise these various functions of government we do not know. We may be sure, however, that they were derived from the Carolingian regalia. In other words, eleventh-century Flanders was actually a miniature kingdom; for its ruler, although he wore no royal crown, was able to enforce such rights as had been abandoned by Charles the Bald and his successors.

Enforcement, inevitably, was the crucial problem, and in Flanders it was solved through a territorial organization that had apparently been perfected during the tenth century. For both civil and military purposes the county was divided into *châtellenies*—districts constructed about castles, such as those of Ghent, Bruges, Ypres, Saint-Omer, Lille, and Arras. Each of these districts was entrusted to a *châtelain*, who in all respects acted as the count's deputy and for that reason was often styled *vicomte* (viscount). He thus commanded the garrison of knights supplied by the surrounding fiefs and saw to it that

---

[1] See above, p. 60.

the castle was stocked with food and other necessities. In the event of war he attended to the summoning of troops from within the *châtellenie* and directed their activities. By way of ordinary routine he also superintended the collection of whatever revenues the count obtained from the district: manorial income, subsidies, tolls, and the like. Upon the *châtelain*, finally, devolved the important duty of holding the territorial court that met inside the castle to administer the count's justice. Although the office of *châtelain* was not at first hereditary, it had usually become so by the middle of the twelfth century. The holders, being rewarded with rich fiefs adjacent to their respective castles, ranked high in the feudal aristocracy. If they had been chronically disobedient, Flanders would have lacked all political stability. That they remained generally faithful was due, not to any theory of vassalage, but to effective control by the count.

Anjou

To the south of Normandy Anjou provided another example of a well-knit feudal state under the remarkable Fulk Nerra and Geoffrey Martel (987–1060). That county, too, was defended and governed by means of castles—among them the earliest known to have had stone towers— which were regularly placed in the keeping of important vassals. And, as in Flanders, such *châtelains* were usually held to a strict loyalty. It was not until the later eleventh century that a disputed succession allowed many of them to get out of hand; then, under Geoffrey Plantagenet (1129–51), the count's authority was again sternly enforced. From reading various standard books one might suppose that feudalism was no more than a form of anarchy. But feudal anarchy was neither constant nor universal in eleventh-century France; the validity of the expression depends altogether on what state is being considered. So far as centralized administration was concerned, Aquitaine was rather a loose union of principalities than a single one. Toulouse had a very turbulent history throughout the Middle Ages. Blois and Champagne never attained the political strength of Flanders and Anjou. Yet none of these territories experienced the disorder that generally characterized the duchy of Burgundy, which, in the absence of all ducal control, was continually fought over by a horde of local barons. Similar conditions prevailed in Brittany and wherever else a theoretical ruler had ceased to rule—even in the royal domain before the accession of the vigorous Louis VI.

How greatly the Normans profited by the experience of their neighbors appears from the structures they had erected by the end of the eleventh century. It is well known that England, under William the Conqueror and his sons (1066–1135), was not only the strongest but also the most thoroughly feudalized state of western Europe. And the more we learn about the early government of Normandy the better we realize that English feudalism was by no means so peculiar as has often been alleged. The fact that William's duchy, as well as his kingdom, was a conquered territory helps to explain why Norman institutions were somewhat more uniform than had come to exist in most of the French principalities. Throughout Normandy, for instance, the substitution of feudal tenure for other forms of landholding seems to have been remarkably complete, and the definition of feudal service in precise quotas of knights to have been especially early. In general, however, the ducal rights were very much the same as those enjoyed by the count of Flanders. The duke nominated prelates, received their homage, and acted as their lay protector. Except by his special authorization, no one in Normandy could build a castle, coin money, regulate sea trade, or hold trials in more serious cases. Formal warfare—as distinguished from the customary prosecution of local feuds—was a monopoly of the duke, who in time of need could summon all able-bodied men of the duchy by proclaiming the *arrière ban*. His authority, finally, was enforced through officials called viscounts as in Flanders, although they were really ducal agents—prominent vassals who had charge of the duke's castles and acted as his deputies for military, judicial, and fiscal administration in the surrounding districts (*vicomtés*).

Feudalism, according to the definition given in a previous chapter, was unknown in England before the Norman Conquest. The Anglo-Saxons, it is true, had been familiar with grants of immunity and with various forms of conditional landholding and personal lordship; but they had never developed a professional class of knights or a plan of rewarding vassals with military benefices. If we leave out of account the few Norman adventurers who had been brought over by Edward the Confessor, it was Duke William and his followers who first established in Britain feudal tenure, feudal warfare, feudal castles, and feudal custom generally. Thus suddenly England was turned into a feudal state patterned after the duchy of Normandy; and the reason for the

The feudalization of England

transformation is clear. The Conqueror substituted what he regarded as the best form of political organization for one that had proved inefficient. Although he preserved such native institutions as he thought might be useful, they were fitted into a new and essentially feudal structure. To him, at any rate, feudalism seemed quite compatible with strong monarchy—an opinion whose justification is surely to be found in the history of the kingdom for the next two hundred years.

The Norman Conquest established the legal principle that every bit of England, if not retained in the king's hands, was held of him as part of some fief—by knight service, by serjeanty, or in free alms.[2] As a consequence, the ruling class throughout the kingdom became a feudal aristocracy which, almost to a man, was Norman-French. The holders of royal fiefs were of course the king's vassals or, as they were technically styled, barons. Thanks to the famous Domesday inquest of 1086, we have a virtually complete catalogue of William's tenants-in-chief, together with a detailed description of their properties. At the bottom of the list we find the relatively insignificant men who possessed only a

---

[2] See above, p. 35.

manor or two; at the top the bishops, abbots, and lay nobles who, after endowing numerous vassals of their own, were left with scores of manors in demesne.[3] Most of these barons, even the ecclesiastics, owed the king quotas of knights which had been assessed against their fiefs immediately after the Norman Conquest. But feudal grants could also be made to remunerate persons who served the king in other ways, notably the chief members of his household. A remarkable document from the early reign of Stephen (1135–54) shows that the heart of the royal court was a group of domestic officials many of whom held their fiefs by serjeanty. Besides, the record tells us, the chancellor, the treasurer, the steward, the butler, the constable, and their principal subordinates were entitled to regular meals at the king's expense, as well as to liveries of bread, wine, and candles, which of an evening they might take to their own quarters.[4]

To safeguard his frontiers, the Conqueror followed a Norman precedent by entrusting them to powerful vassals styled counts. Upon the

William's policy

---

[3] See above, p. 28. Excerpts from Domesday Book, as well as various documents illustrative of feudalism in England, will be found translated in C. Stephenson and F. G. Marcham, *Sources of English Constitutional History* (New York, 1937), Sect. II.

[4] *Ibid.*, no. 29.

Welsh border, for instance, he established three such counts—called earls by the native English —and delegated to them whatever authority he would otherwise have had in the regions about Chester, Shrewsbury, and Hereford. Although principalities of this sort remained exceptional in England, scores of other fiefs carried with them the right of erecting castles and so could be regarded by the king as important units for the defense of his realm. Indeed, according to recognized feudal custom, every fief-holder enjoyed a considerable amount of political privilege. As a minimum, he had limited powers of justice, police, and economic control over the peasants on his estates; and if he had vassals of his own, he could summon them to court for the settlement of disputes affecting their tenures. In one way or another the king thus allowed his barons and their vassals to exercise numerous functions of government. Yet throughout both England and Normandy he asserted a broad claim to judicial and military supremacy. Certain cases were normally reserved for his jurisdiction—known as pleas of the sword in Normandy, as pleas of the crown in England. Any landholder, whether the king's vassal or not, could be required to swear fealty to him; for war could be lawfully waged only in his name, and whenever necessary he could demand service from all able-bodied men (Anglo-Saxon *fyrd*, French *arrière ban*).

In both countries, too, William employed much the same means to enforce his rights. The English kingdom had anciently been divided into shires, each of which was administered by a sheriff, the subordinate of a provincial governor styled *ealdorman* or earl. After the Norman Conquest the earls ceased to have important functions of government except, as already remarked, on certain frontiers. Most of the shires, henceforth also known as counties, were placed under new officials appointed by the king and directly responsible to him. While the English called these officials sheriffs, the French called them viscounts, for they decidedly resembled the men who bore that title on the continent. The Norman sheriff, unlike his Saxon predecessor, was a member of the feudal aristocracy, a great baron whose office, though not formally hereditary, might be passed on to his son. Within his district the sheriff acted as the king's military lieutenant and normally as the custodian, or constable, of a royal castle—one whose construction he had perhaps supervised. In addition he presided over the county court, attended to various matters of police, collected the royal revenues, and carried out the king's orders generally. It is thus obvious that after 1066 the local government of England was brought into close agreement with that of Normandy and Flanders. Such peculiarities as might still be displayed by the English territorial courts or by the English fiscal system were of only minor significance.

The king and his vassals

Anybody who studies the legal and constitutional development of England must realize at the outset that one of his principal concerns is feudalism; for whatever institution of the Norman monarchy he examines is found to have depended on the king's relationship to his barons. It was, of course, from the fiefs of his vassals that the king got practically his entire army and —in the form of aids, feudal incidents, and hospitality—a good portion of his income. It was his vassals who made up his central courts, acted as his permanent ministers, defined his law, and, in one way or another, controlled the local administration of his kingdom. Without the vigorous support of his barons the Conqueror's government could have had no permanence. In England, as in Normandy, he was faced with occasional revolts on the part of discontented minorities; but he was always strong enough to re-establish order, because most of his vassals continued to be loyal. William II and Henry I likewise ruled effectively, and for the same reason. The anarchy under Stephen was the logical result of the king's incompetence. Henry II, finally, was able to restore the system of his grandfather and on the basis of that restoration to make the experiments and improvements for which he has remained illustrious.

In France, meanwhile, the great revival of the monarchy had been begun by Louis VI (1108–37). His first task, as he seems clearly to have realized, was to enforce his authority throughout the royal domain. At his accession the Capetian principality, like the West Frankish kingdom itself, was hardly more than a tradition. Following the example of the great barons, the king's petty vassals in and about the Île de France generally ignored or defied him. On all sides his *prévôts* and *châtelains* conducted their offices to suit themselves, usurping his functions of government, appropriating his revenues, and refusing him admittance to his own castles. To remedy the situation the corpulent but energetic Louis rallied a number of ecclesiastics and other local vassals to his support and took the field at the head of a small army. Eventually the rebels

Restoration of the Capetian principality

were beaten, unauthorized castles were torn down, and disobedient officials were replaced. As a consequence, Louis bequeathed to his successors a firmly organized feudal state—the solid nucleus of the new French kingdom which they built by gradually taking over the neighboring principalities. Regarded from this point of view, feudalism is seen to have been fundamental to the French, as it was to the English, constitution.

Feudalism in Germany and Italy

During the tenth and eleventh centuries, while the kingdom of the West Franks was broken into a series of local states, that of the East Franks seemed to attain increasing solidarity. The kings of the Saxon-Franconian house checked the tendency of the German duchies to become feudal principalities after the French model and successfully enforced the principle that a duke held his office at the royal pleasure, not as a hereditary fief. Within each duchy the king preserved the right to have numerous vassals of his own—especially the great ecclesiastics, whose power was constantly enhanced to offset that of the secular baronage. And in various other ways the rulers of Germany sought to maintain the Carolingian tradition of a grandiose monarchy. They even revived the imperial title and made brave efforts to reign on both sides of the

Alps. But the task was an impossible one. The Holy Roman Empire became a mere sham; and as the prolonged contest between the royal and the princely authority ended in the complete victory of the latter, Germany, like the France of an earlier day, was resolved into a group of feudal states. Although the culmination of this development came only in the later Middle Ages, the German territories had been generally feudalized before the close of the twelfth century. From the Rhinelands to the Slavic frontier armies were made up of knights, society was dominated by a chivalrous aristocracy, the countryside was dotted with motte-and-bailey castles, and governments were organized on the basis of feudal tenure.

In the case of Germany, it may be noted, there was no royal domain to serve as the nucleus of a reconstructed monarchy. Vainly trying to be Roman emperors, the successors of Otto I disdained the possibility of being Saxon, Franconian, or Suabian dukes; the kingship, as it became purely elective, degenerated into a sort of decoration to be borne first by one local prince and then by another. Under such conditions it is quite understandable why feudalism could not be turned, as in France, to the advantage of the crown. And the other component kingdoms of the Holy Roman Empire, Burgundy and Italy, had even less solidarity. For the practical working of feudalism in those regions one must likewise examine the political organizations perfected by royal vassals. In southern Italy, on the contrary, the twelfth-century kingdom of Sicily was as well-knit a state as contemporary England. The reason, of course, was that both countries had been conquered by talented Normans who were able to establish strong governments by shrewdly combining their own feudal custom with whatever native institutions they found useful. The Sicilian kingdom thus owed much to Greek and Saracen precedent; yet its military system, together with various other features of its central administration, was squarely based on feudal tenure.

Additional examples of feudal practice can be *Feudalism in the borderlands of Europe* discovered in large number along the borders of the lands already mentioned—as in Spain, the British Isles, Scandinavia, and the kingdoms of eastern Europe. To avoid wearisome enumeration, it need only be remarked that in all such regions feudalism was generally adopted as a means of political integration. Through the establishment of feudal bonds the German kings continuously sought to extend their control over the semi-barbarous rulers of frontier territories; and those rulers, for all their dislike of German lordship, might well adopt a smiliar method for strengthening their authority over their own subjects. The complicated relationships of the English kings to their neighbors in Scotland, Wales, and Ireland were governed by very much the same considerations; on every side the introduction of feudal tenure marked the advance of Norman influence, if not of Norman conquest. So too in Spain each of the Christian princes built up his little state by enlisting vassals and rewarding them with fiefs at the expense of the Moslems. And this was also the plan of Emperor Alexius when he assembled a crusading host at Constantinople in 1096. That his plan failed was due, not to its impracticality, but to his own bad management.

The kingdom of Jerusalem has often been hailed as the ideal feudal state—one consciously erected according to pure feudal theory and one in which the royal power was therefore reduced to a minimum. In reality, however, that kingdom was at most an afterthought. The original states of the crusaders were those created by the various leaders in the course of a rather haphazard oc-

Feudalism in Syria

cupation of the Syrian coast. After the general repudiation of Alexius, they recognized no common lord and, under ecclesiastical pressure, only agreed to accept one on such terms as they dictated themselves. The result, naturally enough, was the elevation of a titular king who could do little more than carry out the decisions of his greater vassals. But the latter held to no such principle of honorary lordship within their own states, some of which—notably the principality of Antioch—long persisted as independent units. In other words, the kingdom of Jerusalem was weak because it was intended to be so, not because the crusaders were enamored of feudal abstraction. Wherever we encounter feudal institutions, either in Asia or in Europe, they appear to have been developed in response to actual needs. To regard feudalism as something apart from practical politics is utterly to misunderstand the life of the Middle Ages.[5]

---

[5] The author hopes to support at least some of the opinions expressed in this chapter by soon publishing a more specialized article, "Feudalism and Its Antecedents in England."

Chapter Six

THE DECAY OF FEUDALISM

FEUDAL institutions, as we have seen, arose under and generally presupposed an agrarian organization of society. Thanks to feudal tenure, a ruler in the early Middle Ages could obtain a force of expert cavalry, garrison his castles, and provide for all ordinary needs of government without the expenditure of cash. But a state thus feudalized was perforce dominated by the fief-holding class—the great manorial lords who enjoyed a virtual monopoly of wealth. Once that monopoly was broken, feudal arrangements would cease to be necessary. When supplied with money from new sources, a prince would naturally prefer to hire troops and officials in order to increase his personal control of the army and civil administration. The feudal aristocracy, however bitterly it opposed the change, would find

The revival of commerce and the results

97

itself helpless; sooner or later it would lose its
military and political ascendancy.

The decay of feudalism can therefore be understood as one phase of the economic revolution
experienced by western Europe between the
eleventh and thirteenth centuries. In the earlier
period commerce had been reduced to little more
than the local exchange of surplus produce; now,
for reasons that must here be passed over, it was
revived on a large scale. This revival was accompanied by a remarkable increase of the population. Wherever trade flourished, towns rapidly
developed in the course of the twelfth century;
and on all sides the town-dwelling class, or
bourgeoisie, was generally characterized by its
freedom from feudal and manorial bonds, as well
as by its wealth in cash. Spreading from the
towns, the influence of money economy soon
came to be felt in every segment of state and
society. Not even the ancient routines of agriculture and village life could remain untouched. But
long before the average feudal noble was seriously
affected by changes in agrarian organization he
had reason to be concerned with the maintenance
of his political privilege.

Directly or indirectly, the ruling princes of
the twelfth century gained a handsome profit

from the growth of trade throughout their territories, and their improved financial condition *The*
permitted them to establish numerous measures *political*
which their greater vassals soon found dangerous. *decline*
In England, for example, Henry II (1154–89) *feudal*
proved especially adept at strengthening the royal *aristoc-*
administration and at undermining the power of *racy:*
the baronage. He largely increased his revenues *England*
from the towns through taxation and the sale of
special liberties. By inducing his tenants-in-chief
to substitute money payments for their owed
services, he was able to make more frequent use
of mercenary troops. He gradually introduced a
series of judicial reforms, the result of which
was to attract cases into his own courts and away
from those of his barons. In his central government feudal retainers of the old type were generally displaced by professional administrators,
sometimes of bourgeois extraction; and, after his
Inquest of Sheriffs in 1170, similar men were
placed in charge of the counties. The exercise
of political authority in all localities—by the
holders of important fiefs as well as by the sheriffs
—was brought under an ever-tightening super-
vision on the part of the king's itinerant justices.

The threat of royal absolutism, aggravated by
the infamous conduct of John, produced the

barons' revolt of 1215 and the extortion from the
king of *Magna Carta*. But neither that famous
charter nor the subsequent attempts of the baronage to enforce it could restore the dominance of
the feudal aristocracy. The English constitution
that emerged under the Edwards (1272–1377),
though it retained certain feudal elements, was
no logical development of feudalism. By the
fourteenth century the common law, which was
essentially royal, had won a decisive victory over
whatever law was earlier enforced in baronial
courts. The king's ordinary government, both
central and local, was an outgrowth of that de-
vised by Henry II. The English army, despite its
inclusion of many knights, had definitely ceased
to be feudal. Rather it was a mercenary force in
which the mounted noble, as well as the yeoman
archer, humbly served at the king's wages. For
the royal income was likewise independent of the
traditional service from fiefs. The normal tax
was now an assessment upon all men of property
without regard to distinctions of tenure. Such
taxes were regularly voted by spokesmen of the
interested classes in parliament—an enlarged royal
council where the barons, as such, constituted
one of two houses. And even in this one, the
house of lords, only the greater barons came to

have seats, and so to be officially ranked as peers. The English nobility was therefore of parliamentary origin; it was the English gentry, the landed families of the counties, who more truly maintained what was left of the feudal tradition.

In France, despite many developments in common with England, no assembly like the parliament of that country gained constitutional permanence and the feudal aristocracy as a whole preserved its noble status until the Revolution of 1789. But in the meantime this ancient nobility was stripped of political power. As early as the reign of Philip IV (1285–1314) the royal government was largely controlled by bourgeois lawyers and accountants—members of the class whose financial support enabled the succeeding kings, notably Louis XI (1461–83), to throw off the last vestiges of feudal restraint. By the close of the Middle Ages France had thus become an absolute monarchy, and the French example was quickly followed by the rulers of most neighboring territories. Germany, of course, had now been broken into a horde of little states, each of which clung to whatever custom it preferred. So the later history of German feudalism is an appallingly complicated subject. In the present connection it need only be remarked that feudal

France and the continent

institutions, being of comparatively late growth along the eastern frontier, tended to flourish there long after they had virtually died out in the west.

Changes in warfare

To the decline of the feudal aristocracy various military changes of the later Middle Ages gave added impetus. Since the Carolingian age cavalry had become almost the exclusive arm of European princes because it was so vastly superior to any infantry then available. By the end of the thirteenth century, however, conditions were very different. Rulers were now able to pay their troops and, as a consequence, to hold them to a new standard of discipline. Within the mercenary army bodies of foot-soldiers, specially trained and equipped, proved to have great value. It was demonstrated in numerous battles that masses of pikemen could solidly withstand cavalry charges; that longbowmen and crossbowmen, since their arrows would easily penetrate ordinary mail, could be used to good effect for defense or for offense. These lessons in warfare, though not always appreciated at the time, eventually inspired a new tactical system in which the feudal warrior had no place. The knight, it is true, found better protection against archers by covering his body with iron plates.

which were finally joined to form a complete suit. But such armor, in turn, was rendered obsolete by the perfection of fire-arms.

Whatever may be decided with regard to gunpowder, the gun seems to have been a European invention. It is first heard of in the fourteenth century, as a heavy metal tube from which a ball of stone was hurled by means of an explosive charge. A weapon of this sort, even after it had been somewhat improved, was of little worth on the battlefield, and another hundred years had passed before hand-guns were at all effective. In the meantime, however, cannon acquired decisive importance in siegecraft—an art which had lagged far behind that of fortification. By the close of the thirteenth century the castle was no longer an isolated tower encircled by a wall, but an integrated structure, provided with rounded bastions that commanded all parts of the foundation, and subdivided into units that could be separately defended. Such a fortress could be taken only by the slow method of starvation until, in the fifteenth century, moats and masonry were rendered useless by artillery fire. Since then the castle, as is implied by the French word *château*, has been a palatial residence rather than a stronghold.

How these changes in warfare affected the social position of the knight should be obvious. His military, together with his political, dominance was irretrievably lost. Yet the feudal aristocracy, with the decay of its actual power, the more proudly flaunted its chivalrous traditions. Throughout the fourteenth and fifteenth centuries the rage for tournaments, armorial decorations, and other superficial perquisites of the noble class constantly increased—to be reflected in the romantic and pseudo-historical literature of the day. Such vicious kings as Philip VI of France and Edward III of England vied with one another in holding extravagant pageants, establishing knightly orders, and fighting foolish wars. In 1520 Francis I and Henry VIII could still dazzle their subjects with jousts on the Field of the Cloth of Gold. But by that time true chivalry was as obsolete as castles, plate armor, and knight service; even the traditional manor was little more than a memory in the progressive regions of the west.

Decadent chivalry

From the very beginning the growth of a mercantile population in the towns had enormously increased the demand for food and raw materials. And since this demand had led to the rapid improvement of facilities for the sale and distribu-

Vestiges of feudalism

tion of produce, agriculture had tended to become a profitable business. New villages were established by offering attractive terms to settlers, and the success of such undertakings inspired many landlords to reorganize their old villages by commuting all peasant services into cash rents. The result, by the end of the sixteenth century, was the disappearance throughout England and most French provinces of the ancient manorial system, together with the related institution of serfdom. When first made, the substitution of lump sums for the personal obligations of rural tenants was presumably to the advantage of the landlord class. No one could then foresee that a fixed money rent would lose most of its value as increased production of gold and silver reduced the purchasing power of those metals. The calamitous result was left to be experienced by the French nobility of the Old Régime. Under Louis XIV the unhappy aristocrat, being excluded from trade, had to choose between utter impoverishment and courtly servitude at the king's bounty. It was a sorry remnant of the feudal system that the National Assembly abolished in October, 1789.

One who dotes on feudal survivals will hardly bother with France, where nothing remains of the old order except a few noble titles ignored by the law. And in most continental states he will feel that revolutions of one sort or another have rudely disturbed the mediaeval tradition. In England, on the contrary, his search will be handsomely rewarded. There he may be awed by the venerable house of lords, directly descended from the baronial parliament of the thirteenth century—though almost none of the existing peerages antedate the Tudor accession (1485) and most of them are party creations of the last two hundred years. Our sentimental investigator may also be entranced by the pageantry of the British court, with its glitter of heralds, knights, household retainers, and miscellaneous lords and ladies. If he is fortunate enough to witness a royal coronation, he may see the routine splendor made even more splendid by the revival, *pro tem.*, of various hereditary serjeanties. Finally, should his zeal remain unslaked, he may profitably study the chivalrous convictions of the aristocracy: for instance, that a gentleman must be a member of the landed gentry. Few such gentlemen, to be sure, can now expect to attain knighthood; for that has become a special honor conferred by the king to satisfy the peculiar needs of the party in power. Yet men of good family can at least insist upon their eligibility for *adoubement* by reserving to their names the honorable appendage of "Esq."

Thus the *Shorter Oxford English Dictionary:* "Esquire. . . . [See also Squire.] . . . A young man of gentle birth, an aspirant to knighthood, who attended on a knight, and carried his shield. . . . A title allowed by courtesy to all who are regarded as gentlemen." *Honi soit qui mal y pense!*

ON THE general nature of feudalism little has recently appeared in English aside from summaries in various textbooks: notably, J. W. Thompson, *Economic and Social History of the Middle Ages* (New York, 1928), chs. xxv–xxvi, and *The Middle Ages* (New York, 1932), ch. xxiv. The well-known accounts by G. B. Adams, *Civilization during the Middle Ages* (New York, 1922), ch. ix, and C. Seignobos, *The Feudal Régime* (translated from the French by E. W. Dow; New York, 1902), were both written in the nineteenth century and, though still useful, are somewhat out of date. The *Cambridge Medieval History*, unfortunately, includes no adequate discussion of feudalism. And for the moment there is no hope of seeing English translations of the excellent little book by J. Calmette, *La société féodale* (Paris, 1938), or of the two admirable volumes on the same subject by M. Bloch (Paris, 1939–40). For an analysis of other pertinent works, especially those by famous continental scholars, the reader is referred to C. Stephenson, "The Origin and Significance of Feudalism," *American Historical Review*, XLVI, 788–812.

Our libraries are, of course, plentifully supplied with books on costume, arms and armor, castles, knighthood, and other aspects of mediaeval life. Yet few of these books can be expected to pay much attention to early feudal custom, or even to distinguish it from what followed. A welcome exception is provided by S. Painter's *French Chivalry* (Baltimore, 1940), which will be found entertaining as well as historically sound; older writers on chivalry commonly preferred the ideas of romantic or ecclesiastical writers to the conduct of actual knights. Ella S. Armitage gives a fine description of the motte-and-bailey castle, with scores of illustrative diagrams, in her *Early Norman Castles of the British Isles* (London, 1912). For good introductions to military architecture and warfare in the Middle Ages generally, see the chapters by A. H. Thompson in the *Cambridge Medieval History*, vol. VI; also the attached bibliographies. The significance of feudalism in the constitutional history of the European monarchies is a subject that can hardly be understood without a good deal of specialized study, and no attempt to list works in foreign languages can be made here. Any one who is at all familiar with Norman England, however, may profitably examine *The First Century of English Feudalism*, a series of lectures by F. M. Stenton (Oxford, 1932).

So far as contemporary sources are concerned, a number of recommendations have been made, directly or indirectly, in the preceding chapters. The books cited above, p. 18, n. 1, and p. 87, n. 3, contain useful selections of documents to illustrate feudalism. The Bayeux Tapestry has been reproduced in color and provided with a running commentary (not always accurate) by H. Belloc, *The Book of the Bayeux Tapestry* (London, 1914). The *Song of Roland* may be read in several English versions, including one in spirited verse by C. K. Scott-Moncrieff (London, 1920). A splendid example of the more brutal *chansons de geste* is *Raoul de Cambrai*, which has been translated by J. Crosland (London, 1926).

Index